Rober

At the
THE ' _ıH

Priesthood &
Ascetic Life

Robert Cardinal Sarah

At the Service of
THE TRUTH

*Priesthood &
Ascetic Life*

*All books are published
thanks to the generosity of the supporters
of the Catholic Truth Society*

Cover: *Cardinal Sarah* © Bob Roller/CNS;
Procession of priests © Mazur/*catholicnews.org.uk*

Translated by Matthew Sherry
from the Original Italian Edition *A Servizio della Verità*
published by Fede & Cultura, Via Marconi,
58c-60a – 37122 Verona, Italy,
www.fedecultura.com

ISBN 978 1 78469 745 7

Contents

Preface

by Fr Vincenzo Nuara, OP

*Moderator of the Summorum Pontificum
Priestly Friendship Society*

For about three years, because of his many commitments of office and ministry, I had been "chasing" Cardinal Sarah to get him to preach a course of spiritual exercises at the annual retreat of the *Summorum Pontificum Priestly Friendship Society*. Thanks be to God, I finally worked it into his schedule. The texts presented in this volume are the fruit of the work Cardinal Sarah did to provide reflections for the priests at the February 2020 retreat. This was a deep and intimate experience of faith and priestly fellowship.

The path outlined in these pages is the classic one of ascesis as applied to priestly life. This path is not often taken today, unfortunately; little or nothing is said about it. Could a priest live his life without personal, ongoing, and solid ascesis? For all spiritual men of the past and also for Cardinal Sarah, this is not possible. The priestly ministry has a deeply beneficial effect in the personal life and in the apostolate only for those who practise, in their state of life lived out in grace and responsibility, the corresponding ascesis. In short, it can be said that a priest who does not cultivate an authentic ascetic life of prayer and intimate union with God is living an impoverished priesthood that over time can become merely pragmatic, without any yearning for mission and for the supernatural dimension that Christ and the Church entrusted to him on the day of his ordination.

We speak of supernatural mission, because the priest is who he is because he has been called by Christ in a special way for the salvation of the souls he is to sanctify through preaching and sacrament: "I did not come to call the just, but sinners to conversion", the Lord says (*Mk* 2:17). He also commands his disciples: "Go preach the gospel to every creature" (*Mk* 16:15). The Church has received from her divine Master the instruments of sacramental grace, which in Christ's name and by his mandate she confers in priestly ordination upon men chosen and called by God for this holy, distinctive, and unique mission on this earth.

Priesthood and ascesis is the theme of these meditations. But what is asceticism? What is ascesis? It is a personal path of purification, of meditation, of penance, of prayer, of mortification, of renunciation, of intellectual and moral discipline, of ongoing self-examination, of interior growth. In a word: it is an itinerary of life, an inward path for reaching full

conformity with Christ, imitating his intimate
relationship with the Father in prayer and silent
recollection; and, for a priest, with Christ the good
shepherd and victim of love. St Thomas Aquinas
affirms that ascesis tends to perfect man's relationship
with God: this perfection matures through love
(cf. *Summa Theologiae*, II-II. q. 24 a. 9). We could
therefore say that ascesis is an act of love expressed
every day in an intense life of prayer before God in
loving contemplation and adoration; without this,
the minister of God can risk living his priestly life
as just another profession, albeit a noble one, in an
exclusively human, almost philanthropic way without a
contemplative and consequently apostolic longing. The
gospel he preaches must be in his life, as well as on
his lips with preaching, so he may not be reproached
on account of his inconsistent and unsound life, as
St Paul recalls (cf. *1 Co* 9:27). The priest is therefore
the mouth of God: *os Domini*, first with the evangelical
witness of his life and then with his words. The cardinal
continues: "The asceticism that is imposed on us consists
in learning true priestly freedom in saying and doing that
which allows Christ, whose unworthy representatives
we are, to shine through our speech and our actions".

The emphasis in seminaries on the human dimension
of ministry, advanced by a horizontalist, exclusively
anthropocentric theology, has impoverished the
priestly formation and spiritual life of many future
priests. This approach has debased and secularised the
life of many priests, who in the long run feel tired and
unmotivated, sometimes burdened by urgent requests

from the hierarchy, by inconsistent and unattainable pastoral plans, and by the demands of the faithful and of parish life with its intense and unsustainable rhythms. The crisis experienced by many priests is based on this functionalist view of the Catholic priesthood rather than on the reality of ecclesiastical celibacy, a claim that some promote with the complicity of the secularist mass media.

Ascesis helps give the priest a realistic and concrete view of his abilities and his moral and spiritual strengths, and at the same time helps him, accompanied by a good spiritual father, to make decisions beneficial and essential for his own path of sanctification and for that of the souls entrusted to him in the ministry. The priest must realise that since it is not necessary or even possible for him to do everything, his duty is rather to choose the "better part…" (cf. *Lk* 10:41-42) and bring this to the attention of the faithful and, also, to his own attention: "We must leave behind many of our past habits in order to make room for our Christological representation above all else", the cardinal continues.

Cardinal Sarah has stated that he had nothing new to say in these meditations. I think rather that, like the *good scribe* of the parable, he was able to draw from the Holy Gospel and from the venerable Tradition of the Church *old things and new things* useful for living our priestly life today, so beset on every side.

On behalf of all, I would like to thank him for the beautiful and profound meditations and for the time he has given us, together with his edifying and simple presence: this will be a memory that we will carry forever in our souls. I am sure that reading these pages will do a great deal of good for priests and will sustain them in the battle of daily and loving fidelity to Christ and his Mystical Bride. But it will also be nourishing for lay readers, in the ongoing discovery of the beauty of the priesthood that Our Lord has left to his Church for our edification and salvation.

Rome, Ash Wednesday, 17th February 2021

Introduction to the Spiritual Exercises

Dearest brother priests,

With this brief introduction, we begin our journey through the Spiritual Exercises. The Exercises represent a very important moment in the life of a priest. The priest is a minister of Christ, that is, a servant of Christ. Servants can be good or bad, as our Master recalls in the famous Gospel parable (cf. *Mt* 24:45-51; *Lk* 12:35-55). Of course, it is true that a bad servant is still a servant. In this sense we do not lose the service, the ministry, meaning that we would not lose the priesthood if unfortunately we should occasionally fall into mortal sin, or worse, live permanently outside the grace of God. All the same we would remain priests. Bad ministers, but still ministers.

However, we know very well that this objective nature of the ministry received must not represent an excuse. It is true that even if the priest is in mortal sin, the acts he performs in his ministry are valid if the elements necessary for validity are respected. But no priest should quiet his conscience on this account, saying, "Even if I live badly, I am still serving the Lord." It is true that the sacraments he celebrates are valid and confer grace on the faithful. But he will have to give an account of his stewardship to the just Judge. And those who have received much will have to answer to a more severe judgement. We have received much, very much indeed. According to some authors – excluding the graces reserved exclusively for one person, for example the privileges of Mary Most Holy – the vocation to the priesthood is the greatest grace that God can give a human being. Whether this opinion is correct or not, we are confident in saying that the vocation to the priesthood is, at the very least, one of the greatest graces that God can grant to a man. Already this evening, then, let us prepare to examine ourselves during these Spiritual Exercises. We will have to ask ourselves many times during these days: "How do I live my priesthood? How do I respond to this extraordinary grace that the Lord, in total gratuitousness and really without any merit of mine, has granted me?" Let us think about it, brothers. Let us think about how high this divine election is. Let us remember that the Lord has thought of each of us from all eternity. From eternity he decided, in his infallible decree, that we were to be sacramentally identified with Jesus Christ, conformed to him through sacred priestly ordination. From eternity God the Father wanted us to be, in a certain sense, not just *alter Christus*, but even *ipse Christus*, Christ himself on earth. But are we aware of this gift? And how do we respond to it?

During these days, God willing, we will carry out some reflections on our priestly life. Much if not indeed all I have to say you have already heard. During the years of our seminary studies and then later during the years of our ministry we read many books, attended many lectures…somehow it seems we have already heard it all. Perhaps that is so. Perhaps we already know everything and this course of Spiritual Exercises will not say anything new that we do not already know or have read or heard about from other sources. But let us ask ourselves if, in addition to knowing it, we have also meditated on what we have read and heard. Let us ask ourselves if to mere knowledge we have added contemplation. Let us ask ourselves if the spiritual food has remained – if the metaphor is permitted – in the stomach, or if we have digested and assimilated it, making it our own. Contemplation is to mere knowledge as digestion and metabolism are to merely ingesting food.

Today there are so many sources, so many resources. With the internet we can feed constantly on news and information. We consume knowledge, data, all the time. But then, do we reflect on what we have read? Our body, when we give it ordinary food, digests and metabolises it. Metabolism causes that food, which was a reality different from me, to be transformed into me. Our mind should also metabolise what we hear and read. That is, it should take what is fitting from the things we have learned and heard over again, and make it part of our life. So let us approach these Spiritual Exercises with the desire to meditate and contemplate on the things we already know, so that we may truly know them and therefore also live them.

Let us place ourselves under the mantle of Our Lady. Let us ask her for her protection and her blessing. Let us ask her to support these priest sons of hers during these days, so that the food of the Word of God and of sound doctrine may nourish our souls and sustain us in the ceaseless conversion to God of which we are ever in need.

The Current Situation of Moral and Spiritual Decadence Among the Clergy (Lack of Faith and Zeal)

St John Chrysostom, in his famous treatise on the priesthood, says that – because of the very high dignity they have received – priests must in their moral lives shine brighter than the sun. Given the importance of this teaching, which we will recall a number of times over the coming days, let us consult his exact words: "The soul of the priest must be purer than the sun's rays, so that the Holy Spirit may never abandon him and he may say: 'It is no longer I who live, but Christ who lives in me'" (St John Chrysostom, *On the Priesthood*, VI, 1,504; VI, 2,8-9).

How beautiful it is to contemplate this truth! The priest is Christ's representative on earth. He is not just an "*alter Christus*", but even "*ipse Christus*". Now, one of the aspects of the mystery of Jesus Christ is precisely that of his extraordinary holiness. We all know and believe that the Mother of Jesus is the Immaculate. That Mary is immaculate means that she was protected, in view of the future merits of her Son, from any contagion of sin. She is *sine macula*. Our Lady is therefore venerated with this wonderful title, which expresses a dogma of the faith: the Immaculate Conception. This Marian truth, however, is not always considered in terms of its Christological root. Mary was kept immaculate because she was to give birth to the most pure Son. We can say that Mary is the Immaculate Woman (*Immacolata*) because she was to be the Mother of the true Immaculate Man (*Immaculato*), Christ the Lord. In Christ is the origin of the most perfect holiness. It is he who is the Immaculate Man, and therefore Our Lady is also the Immaculate Woman.

We priests have been made representatives of the Immaculate Man. We know very well that we are not like him, but our vocation implies that, in some way, we should reproduce his spotlessness. This is why Chrysostom said that the priest must shine brighter than the earthly sun: he must in fact shine with the rays of the supernatural sun, Jesus Christ. Let us think of the Marian image of Revelation: the Woman clothed with the sun (*Rv* 12). But that's just it, she is clothed, arrayed with the sun. Mary is not the sun. She is the moon, which reflects the light of the true sun, the *orientale lumen* that is Jesus. The priest is called to let shine upon him the sun that is Christ. The priest is not the sun: no! Christ is. But the priest must be mantled in holiness. In him holiness acts as a mantle-mirror. If he is mantled in this mirror, he will better reflect the rays of the Christological sun. Let us now meditate on this image of the mirror.

We know that St Paul uses it to describe our journey of faith here below. In the first letter to the Corinthians, the apostle says that now we walk by faith and not yet by sight. The Latin version says that we contemplate God and the transcendent realities *per speculum et in aenigmate*. "Now we see in a confused way, as in a mirror; but then we will see face to face. Now I know in an imperfect way, but then I will know perfectly, as I too am known" (*1 Co* 13:12). This is usually translated: "We see as though through a mirror and in a confused way". At first glance, these words seem wrong. When we look in the mirror, we do not see in a confused way at all, but very clearly. Why does St Paul say that looking into a mirror he sees himself in a confused way? In all probability, because St Paul did not have the kind of mirrors we have today. In ancient times the mirror was certainly a very useful tool and one that, all in all, fulfilled its function. However, ancient mirrors were much less functional than current ones. They were surfaces, usually of metal, which were made as even and smooth as possible so as to reflect images. But although the images were visible, they were less clear than those of natural eyesight. The object could be seen, yes, but not very well: it was blurred and the reflected image was opaque. St Paul applies this to faith and says that we see God, we know God already by faith during this life, but not directly (in fact, the mirror gives us an indirect view of an object) and not even clearly (since ancient mirrors did not render a perfect image).

Let us apply these observations to our being priests, called to reflect the sun which is Christ. We have been made a mirror of the holiness of Christ. But our mirror, what condition is it in? Is it smooth, clean, well-polished, so as to give the best possible reflection of the light? Or is it dirty, chipped, dented, so that it hardly reflects a glimmer?

Priestly life has never been easy. But perhaps today it is even less so. The temptations and opportunities to fall into sin are truly many; one could say more so than in the past. And we say "more so than in the past" not because all previous eras were better than ours, but because today there are means and habits, at least in the Western world, that facilitate sin, when they do not positively approve of, promote, and recommend it.

Without claiming to make a complete list, let us try to mention some of these elements that today, more than in the past, put the moral integrity of the priest at risk:

1. The education he received. Today's younger priests have often grown up in families where their parents almost always loved them, but often did not also educate them. In present-day families, for many reasons, there is a great educational void. Children are often left to themselves, when they are not left in bad company, either because both parents work or because, when they come back home, they don't have it in them or don't want to sacrifice the last

hours of the day to being with their children and educating them. That is why young people today get their education (or rather miseducation) from school (too often a venue for ideology), television and the internet, as well as from their peers, who however are in the same situation. From the educational point of view, parents are absent. One of the main causes of this is that today the importance of sacrifice is not understood. Love is thought to be a feeling. A parent may believe he loves his children simply because he feels love for them. But in many cases, it is not understood that loving children means sacrificing one's own time and energy in order to be a consistent presence for them, to correct and even punish them if necessary, so that they may grow up well.

Moreover, even in Catholic families there is often not enough religious education, or none at all. The parish or ecclesial association that the children may attend has an important role, but it cannot replace the essential religious education that is received in the family. And we must add that today even the parish or Catholic associations often do not carry out their educational and formative task well.

So this is the first reason. Many of today's priests did not receive a solid human, affective, and religious education in the family. In particular, they were not raised in the faith from an early age and, above all, they were not educated in the value of renunciation and sacrifice. In large sectors of the younger clergy (let's say aged fifty and under), it is not unusual to see a reluctance to make sacrifices. This reverberates throughout many aspects of the ministry, but also in the field of resisting temptations and seeking the means to strengthen oneself against them, especially the great means of penance.

2. From this follows a second aspect: organisation, the structuring of one's days, the rule of life. Several years ago, a bishop confided that he was rather disturbed about the typical daily schedule of a number of his younger priests. What this bishop was saying seemed hard to believe. Some of his young priests (even if they were parish priests or assistant parish priests, with serious responsibilities) got up no earlier than ten or eleven in the morning. Their church, of course, was closed in the morning. Once the bishop found himself passing through a small village in his diocese and, seeing the church closed when it was almost noon, he asked an old woman on the street the reason for this. And the old woman replied, "The priest is sleeping." And this was not an extraordinary event, but an everyday one. The people of that village knew that in the morning, every morning, the church was closed, that it was not possible to enter to pray, because the priest was sleeping. The bishop then described the rest of the day for such priests: breakfast or lunch around noon; in the early afternoon watching television or posting comments and images on Facebook and other social networks; then phone calls with fellow priests or

get-togethers in person. In both cases, the reason for the conversation is simply to gossip about everything and everyone. The bishop said that such priests can spend more than two hours a day posting videos and texts on social media, many of them ridiculous or meaningless, as well as gossiping with fellow priests. Then, around five or six in the evening, the moment finally comes to open the church to celebrate Mass. After Mass has been celebrated and a few other errands run, the evening ends around eight and the long night begins: outings with friends (some priests even go to nightclubs), going to the cinema or watching television and playing on the computer at home...all without a care in the world until two in the morning.

We repeat: listening to this story, at first one is tempted not to believe it. We know many priests, even among the very young, who do not live like this at all. But after consulting other bishops the reality of the story was confirmed. Again, not all priests are like this, on the contrary! By the grace of God there are many priests, both old and young, who are very dedicated to their ministry and who sacrifice themselves for it. The Lord bless them! But it is unfortunately true that other priests idle their time away: the time that is so precious for serving Christ and the Church and that, once wasted, cannot be recovered, since it is impossible to go back. "The years of our life are seventy, eighty for those who are strong, [...] they pass quickly and we fly away. [...]

Teach us to number our days and we will acquire a wise heart"(*Ps* 90:10, 12).

It is known that the saints did not like to waste time. St Alphonsus Maria de Liguori apparently made a vow never to waste time. We can say that wasting time is truly a sin. It corresponds to the attitude of that man in the parable who, instead of working to multiply the talent he received, went to bury it. That saying is true which says, "idleness is the father of vices". If so many priests are living in sin, this often depends in part on their totally disorganised and truly mistaken daily schedule. We remember that the great David sinned with Bathsheba because at that time he was relaxed, he was living badly, without a good rule of life. While the troops were fighting, while others were giving their lives for Israel, David slept until late afternoon, and after waking up he sauntered out onto the terrace of his house. There the devil found him and easily prevailed over him because, through that way of life, David had dug the pit under his feet; he had stood alone on the edge of the precipice (*2 S* 12:1-15). What then are we to think of the behaviour of those idle priests who, while some of their brethren are giving their lives generously for the cause of the Church, spend their days in dissipation? God forbid that we be among them!

3. A third danger is the aforementioned disorderly use of the internet. There may be no need to point out that we have nothing against the internet itself,

because if used well it is indeed a great resource, including for the Church. But its misuse is harmful. Various websites, blogs and social media platforms are contributing heavily to the current cultural disaster. And we are not referring only to sites of an evidently sinful or ideological character. In a sense those are less dangerous, because there the sin or error is evident, so anyone who wants to avoid sin will also avoid looking at those pages. The true danger of the internet lies elsewhere, in its potential to destroy our brain. In what sense do we make such a serious statement? We say it in the sense that if we allow the internet to replace reflection, our conscience, and our responsibility to discern in the light of Revelation, then we become like automatons in the hands of others.

In and of itself, every learning process requires a form of passivity. There is a teacher or a text that teaches, and there is a pupil who learns. The first movement towards knowledge is primarily passive: allowing reality to enter us so that our intellect can reformulate it in terms of truth. Truth is in fact material reality as comprehended by the mind in an immaterial way. This is the first step in knowledge according to the sound epistemology of philosophical realism: the passive reception of sense impressions and their conceptual elaboration. Then comes the second step. After conceptual understanding, which is obtained through abstraction, the mind can and must perform another operation: judgement. That is, the mind must judge the thing it has comprehended by comparing it with other things. The mind can and must say, "This thing is such and not otherwise, this is true or false", and so on. Here, in the faculty of judgement, the active component of our intellect is displayed on a higher level of conceptual formulation. Let us take up again the metaphor of nutrition that we used before. In eating there is first of all passivity: we receive within us the food that is given to us by someone who has prepared it. But then the body moves into action to metabolise it (or, if the food is rotten, to reject it).

In the age of the internet, we have at our disposal an enormous amount of data and ideas, that is, food for the mind. The point is that the more we read the less we digest. In schools of any level, from elementary to university, instruction always tries to cover both aspects: giving content to students on the one hand, but also getting the students to rework the knowledge received through seminars, written exercises, and preparation for exams. The internet, however, does not require any of this. It gives and, apparently, gives without asking for anything in return. Many today are under the illusion that they know everything, just because they always carry a mobile phone and at any moment can use it to look up information of any kind. But true knowledge is that which is digested, not that which we use and then discard from the mind immediately, as soon as we turn off the computer or phone screen.

Here then is the danger: that the internet may destroy our brain, meaning our critical capacity, the capacity to reason, evaluate, and judge the things we read and see. We thus become puppets in someone else's hands. We follow sensations instead of right reason. Recently the OECD (Organisation for Economic Co-operation and Development), as part of its programme called PISA (*Programme for International Student Assessment*), conducted a survey on the study capacity of present-day students. The results are truly worrying. Without dwelling on the many aspects of this research, we note a fact that is truly frightening: a high percentage of present-day adolescents do not have the ability truly to understand what they read. We know very well that Western countries have very high literacy rates: practically everyone can read and write. Everyone can read, but a good percentage of young people are unable to understand what they read. Teenagers are used to reading short texts, for example a tweet or a text message, but if the composition is any longer than that, they lose focus and cannot follow it any more.

In spite this, the universities continue to churn out graduates. But with the average preparation of these graduates, some of whom fail to understand what they read in their university textbooks, what level will it be at? The concern is great: these are the ranks that in a few years will be producing architects, lawyers, engineers, army officers, diplomats, politicians... what will happen then, considering that already today the social panorama is full of figures that are hardly dazzling in terms of the depth of their specific preparation for their roles?

A priest should live differently. In this age of internet passivity, in this time when people no longer think for themselves, he should avoid the systematic killing of the brain that is perpetrated in this way. Above all, the priest should be a person who thinks, who develops a critical judgement on reality, since he must guide others to recover the reason that today is clouded.

And yet we see that a certain number of priests today, with respect to the internet, behave like everyone else. These ministers of Christ spend a lot of time at the keyboard or with the phone in their hands, posting images and texts that are superficial or ridiculous when they are not downright erroneous in terms of Christian doctrine or scandalous in content. This latter observation leads us to a fourth aspect.

4. The poor theological and doctrinal preparation of many priests also exposes them more easily to sin. It is true that solid preparation is not enough to avoid sin. We have seen that there have also been cases of doctrinally well-rounded priests who were not, however, morally sound. Good doctrine alone, therefore, is not enough to preserve one from sin. But it is true that sound doctrine, combined with other things, is necessary and greatly helps a priest to avoid occasions of sin. We will come back to

this at another time. For now, we would just like to emphasise that every priest has the duty to read and study and, if possible, to read and study good books, books that help him. This too is helpful in leading a life in which we shine like the sun, reflecting the rays of Christ.

We have mentioned just four areas of contemporary life in which priests today may find themselves more exposed to sin. There are others of course, but it seemed appropriate to point these out first. We could perhaps summarise what has been said so far with one word: prudence. To avoid sin one must be prudent. Prudence is the virtue of using good means to reach a good end. Our good end is that of being worthy and holy priests of Jesus. Therefore we must constantly ask ourselves: what means must I use in view of this end? Naturally, just as the end is good, so also must the means be, because in our doctrine the use of bad means is not allowed, not even to attain a good end. The end does not justify the means. Let us try to use good means to reach a good end.

When we go to confession, we have the good habit of reciting the Act of Contrition. In it we say to God: "I firmly resolve, with the help of your grace, to sin no more and to avoid the near occasions of sin". The good end is "to sin no more". This, of course, is possible only with the grace of God and therefore in the same prayer we say: "I firmly resolve, with the help of your grace". In fact, without such help it would be impossible not to sin. However, in addition to grace, human co-operation is needed. So, what are we to do on our part? What means should we use? The prayer says: "I firmly resolve...to avoid the near occasions of sin." We know very well how today many no longer understand the exact meaning of these words. And this is not their fault, but rather ours, because we no longer teach so many beautiful and right things that were taught to us. That is why many today think that the near occasion of sin means a *future* occasion. In fact, this is one of the meanings of the word "near", which can indicate something that comes later. But it is clear that this is not the meaning of the formula we are commenting on here. If this were so, the Act of Contrition would be saying something obvious and even ridiculous: I propose to avoid the occasions of sin that will occur in the future...of course! After all, how could one avoid the occasions that have already occurred in the past?

"Near occasions" cannot mean future occasions, but occasions *bordering* on sin, occasions that lead me to sin, as David's sloth put him in the near occasion of sin and he in fact sinned. The priest, then, must be prudent: he must use good means to keep from getting close to sin. Because sin is like a chained dog: it is scary even from far away, but it bites you only if you come within striking distance. So let us keep prudently away from its striking distance!

PART II

This morning we talked about some dangerous elements for the moral life of today's priest. We identified the general remedy for such dangers in the virtue of prudence. But now we would like to ask ourselves what is the root of the disordered and even sinful life of certain priests. In the first place, we could say that a certain way of living the priesthood stems from a lack of zeal.

We always remember with pleasure how in one of his homilies Benedict XVI took up this beautiful word "zeal". And he did not just say "zeal", but he used the complete expression "zeal for souls", also citing the corresponding Latin *animarum zelus*:

> The last keyword that I should like to consider is "zeal for souls": *animarum zelus*. It is an old-fashioned expression, not much used these days. In some circles, the word "soul" is virtually banned because – ostensibly – it expresses a body-soul dualism that wrongly compartmentalises the human being. Of course the human person is a unity, destined for eternity as body and soul. And yet that cannot mean that we no longer have a soul, a constituent principle guaranteeing our unity in this life and beyond earthly death. And as priests, of course, we are concerned for the whole person, including his or her physical needs – we care for the hungry, the sick, the homeless. And yet we are concerned not only with the body, but also with

the needs of the soul: with those who suffer from the violation of their rights or from destroyed love, with those unable to perceive the truth, those who suffer for lack of truth and love. We are concerned with the salvation of men and women in body and soul. And as priests of Jesus Christ, we carry out our task with enthusiasm. No one should ever have the impression that we work conscientiously when on duty, but before and after hours we belong only to ourselves. A priest never belongs to himself. People must sense our zeal, through which we bear credible witness to the gospel of Jesus Christ. (*In the footsteps of Vatican Council II*, homily at the Chrism Mass on Holy Thursday, 5th April 2012)

What is zeal? It is interest. A person is zealous when someone or something really interests him. Zeal for souls is therefore the interest that the shepherd must take in the eternal salvation of the sheep entrusted to his care.

When we are truly interested in something there is no obstacle that can stop us, there is no weariness that can slow us down, there is no habit that can bore us: we do all we can, strain every fibre of our being in order to obtain it. Zeal for souls does all it can to obtain their eternal salvation by God. As we know, the Holy Curé of Ars is, for us priests, a constant point of reference. When he first came to his new parish someone told him, "You're too late, father, here in Ars there's nothing more to do." To which he replied, "Then there is everything to do!" What he did was to get up at two in the morning (just the time when some priests today are going to sleep!) and to go to church, where he spent long hours in front of the tabernacle meditating, reciting the breviary, praying the Holy Rosary and conversing with the Lord in prayerful silence. Before long so many people were coming to Ars that the poor curate was hard pressed to find the time to continue his prayer life as before.

Zeal for souls motivated the Curé of Ars. It is not by chance that he is the patron saint of all priests who, even with different ministries, commendably dedicate themselves to the care of souls. This, after all, is the origin of the word "curate". The curate is the one who takes care of the faithful. He is the good shepherd who stands front and centre looking after the interests of the flock.

In his homily, Benedict XVI recalled that in recent decades ecclesial language has stopped using the word "soul". To speak of the "care of souls" or "salvation of souls" seemed, to a certain mentality, a mistake (*Mk* 8:36; *Mt* 16:26; *Mk* 3:4). The claim is that since man is made not only of soul but of soul and body, we must speak of the salvation of man or of the person, not of the salvation of the soul. The tragic absence of the word "soul" can also be noted in the new translations of Sacred Scripture. "*Quid enim prodest homini, si mundum universum lucretur, animae vero suae detrimentum pretiatur? Aut quam dabit homo commutationem pro anima sua?*" "Indeed, what advantage will a man have if he gains the whole world, but loses his own life? Or what can a man give in exchange for his own life?" (*Mt* 16:26; *Mk* 8:36.) "*Et dicit eis: Licet sabbati bene facere an male? Animam salvam facere an perdere?"* "Then he asked them: Is it lawful on the Sabbath day to do good or to do evil, to save a life or to kill it?" (*Mk* 3:4.) Also, before communion with the Body and Blood of Christ we say: *Domine, non sum dignus ut intres sub tectum meum, sed tantum dic verbo et sanabitur anima mea.* The Italian version has "O Lord, I am not worthy to participate at your table, but say only one word and I will be saved." You have noticed with dismay and a feeling of disappointment that the word "soul" has been replaced with the word "life". This is a substantial change and in my opinion wrong, because it is disrespectful of the word of God. Although the observation that man is a union of body and soul is obviously correct, we must nevertheless remember that the Council of Vienne accepted into the Church's doctrinal view the philosophical truth according to which the soul is the form of the body. As a result, the soul is the active principle of the human composite and also informs the material part of man. Thus if the soul is saved, so is the body. Besides, it is in the soul that the noblest faculties of the human being are found, those that freely co-operate in salvation. It is therefore still appropriate to express oneself in these terms: salvation of the soul, zeal for souls.

Do we priests have zeal for souls? Are we interested in souls? Are we interested in the eternal destiny of the people we have before us? They certainly interest Christ! He truly had zeal for souls, to the point of paying their ransom with his blood. It is sad to see that some priests seem to have no interest in the eternal salvation of the faithful. They focus entirely on the horizontal plane, trying to solve certain political, economic, social, immigration or environmental problems. Naturally, in these sectors too the Church must make herself heard, within the limits of the tasks that Christ has given her. But the essential, we could say, lies elsewhere. The essential is zeal for souls. Some priests seem to have none or to have lost it. But Christ has it!

How sad it is to see that so many souls may be lost through the coldness, the indifference of those who had been appointed to work together with God for their salvation! We may not be interested in souls, but Christ is! In fact, the souls did not cost us anything, but Christ paid dearly for them. Some priests want only to receive from souls, and not to give. They want the faithful to respect them, esteem them, acclaim them, always back them up, never speak against them, and give everything necessary to support them. And these things in themselves are, generally speaking, also right. But shouldn't priests give anything to souls? They will say, "But I administer the sacraments!" To which one could reply, "Oh, well done. What are you going to do, leave those out as well?" It is true that administering the sacraments is the most important thing, because it is Christ who saves and not the priest. But let us ask ourselves: beyond the duty I have to dispense the sacraments, what of my own do I give for souls? How much more time, how much more effort and perhaps even how much of my financial resources do I put in service of the cause? Am I someone who just wants to receive or do I also want to give?

The good spirit of the priest, which is the spirit of pastoral charity, is expressed well in the famous *Prayer of St Francis of Assisi*: "O Master, let me seek not so much to be understood as to understand, to be loved as to love…"

We were just saying that a priest who has zeal is a priest who puts himself front and centre to defend the flock. This warrior's spirituality of being on the front line is expressed well in the Ignatian approach. St Ignatius founded the Jesuits so that as ardent soldiers of Christ, fighting under his standard, they might stand courageously and without fear in the breach. This spirituality, as we know, was partly born from St Ignatius's own military experiences. He knew very well that a citadel can withstand a siege for a long time if its walls remain standing. (In the case of the Church, it can hold out until the relieving force arrives to drive away the besiegers forever: the Church withstands them until the return of Christ with all the heavenly hosts.) But if the enemy manages to break through, then the city is lost, unless a handful of brave soldiers step into the breach and repel the assault. In the mind of St Ignatius, the Society of Jesus was to be that handful. For centuries this is how it operated. The Jesuits were in the breach, that is, always in the vanguard, with schools, studies, and missions. They were men in the breach who stood on the front line not in order to fall from the walls or facilitate enemy infiltration into the citadel, but to defend its entrance. Standing in the breach, according to St Ignatius, was to repel invaders, a defensive function. One does not stand on the threshold in order to let the enemy in or even to say that the enemy does not exist, that the devil does not exist, and that those who are inside or outside the walls are fundamentally the same. If one reasons in this way, the citadel is doomed.

The zealous priest is a man who places himself in the breach, not to say to the enemy: "Come right in and devastate the vineyard", but rather courageously to repel the assaults. The good shepherd gives his life for his flock. The good shepherd guards the sheepfold and with his crook drives away the wolves and foxes. But if the shepherd were to open the gate to them, the sheep would be sure to die. To be more precise, the shepherd is not able to open the gate, because the gate is Christ and Christ never opens to sin and error. The malevolent shepherd, then, rather than opening the gate, will himself make a breach in the sheepfold, to let evil in among the flock.

To be a good shepherd, a good soldier in the breach, the priest cannot sleep. You know very well we mean this metaphorically. It is obvious that on the literal level we do not recommend foregoing rest. On the contrary, we have to sleep in order to replenish our energy. When we say that the priest cannot sleep, we mean that he must be aware of his mission and must be constantly vigilant. He must be a man who prays, always in front of the tabernacle, like the Curé of Ars, for his sheep. Furthermore, as we said this morning, he must be someone who thinks critically and teaches others to think about what today's world and culture have to offer.

The zealous priest is concerned that the cultural and ideological movements of our time could pollute the souls of his sheep: especially the souls of the youngest, who are still in search of their own vision of the world. And if they are already polluted, the zealous pastor will offer his service as a doctor, trying to eliminate the poison that has infiltrated the thinking of so many Catholics. The Church has a grand vision of the world and of life. This is what Romano Guardini called the Katholische Weltanschauung: the Catholic vision of the world. The zealous priest dedicates himself, through appropriate reading, to cultivating this vision first of all for himself, and then tries to pass it on to others by word and example.

But we can also ask ourselves: what is the root of this kind of zeal? Where does zeal for souls come from? And if someone has lost it or it has grown cold in him, how can he recover it? The same question can also be asked with regard to the negative cases of lack of zeal: what is lacking in those priests who do not have zeal for souls? We can probably answer with just one word: faith. Zeal is lacking because faith is lacking or faith is weak.

The priestly ministry is a ministry of faith. This genitive ("of faith") can be understood in both a subjective and an objective sense. It is an objective genitive, because our ministry has faith as its object. In this sense, the priest is a minister of the Word of God, keeper of the deposit of faith, preacher of revealed truth. But it is also a subjective genitive, meaning that the priesthood is a ministry that is born of faith and is exercised as a consequence of the faith of the one who has been ordained. Therefore, if faith is lacking or weak, the consequences for the ministry will be disastrous.

When we studied basic theological courses, we all learned the classical distinction between *fides qua creditur* and *fides quae creditur*, that is, the faith with which one believes (subjective sense) and the faith that one believes (objective sense). The latter is the doctrine of the faith, while the former is the believer's personal adherence. It should be emphasised that, for Catholic theology, there is a true act of faith only when both of these dimensions are present together. In fact, this is a theological distinction. It is a correct distinction, but in an act of faith these two dimensions, although distinct, must absolutely always be united. If this were not the case, we would have a pseudo-faith, not the true Catholic faith. In fact, one could have good *fides quae*, that is, good doctrinal knowledge. But there still must be existential adherence to the doctrine professed. In recent decades, we have seen a number of cases of priests and laity (some of whom have been founders of new ecclesial institutes and movements) who professed sound faith at the doctrinal level, but were later found guilty of various kinds of abuses: abuse of conscience, abuse of authority, psychological and even physical abuse. On the other hand, we also know many cases of priests who, from a purely subjective point of view, are all in all good people, but in their teaching and in the practical decisions of their ministry do not follow the doctrine of the Church, at least not in all instances. This would be the case of those who perhaps have good *fides qua*, that is, sincerely believe in the Lord and are often even capable of diligent ecclesial work, but whose thinking differs either in whole or only in part from the thinking of Christ. So, in his initiatives such a priest will follow worldly rather than evangelical thinking. In this case he will cause damage both to individual souls and to the Church as a whole, however good his purely subjective intentions may be.

We need priests of faith. But "of faith" according to the complete sense of the category: both *fides qua* and *fides quae creditur*. From faith comes zeal. If the priest adheres with his whole self to Christ and professes the doctrine of the Church without hesitation, this will lead to love for the eternal salvation of souls along with commitment and the willingness to sacrifice in order that the Lord may use his life to save men. After all, it won't cost too much for the priest of true and solid faith – in spite of a few weary moments – to put his life in Jesus's hands and say to him, "Use me, Lord. Take everything. I give you all of me, so that you may use it for your ends." Zeal for souls is, after all, an offshoot of zeal for the Lord, for his cause.

The priest of faith does not perform his duties because he expects to receive something in return. He performs them because he has understood that this is right and beautiful; because he has understood that this is the true meaning of his life. Zeal and zealous action fill his thoughts, his plans, the hours of his days. Work is tiring, it is true! But work done for Christ's sake is at the same time refreshing. In a beautiful prayer, St Ignatius of Loyola has this to say:

Accept, O Lord, my entire liberty, my memory, my understanding, and my will. All that I am and have you have given to me; and I give all back to you to be disposed of according to your good pleasure. Give me only the comfort of your presence and the joy of your love; with these I shall be more than rich and shall desire nothing more.

It is clear that this type of prayer and the spiritual sentiments it expresses can come only from strong faith. Generally speaking, strong faith is instilled in the soul during childhood. That is why this morning we noted the serious harm caused by a lack of religious education in the family. If one does not acquire strong faith as a child, it will be necessary later to make up for lost time, which is ever more difficult, as evidenced for example by how much harder it is to learn a language the older one gets. The mother tongue is the one that is spoken best, with agility of speech, with exact pronunciation and grammatical correctness. The mind of a child is a prodigious mind: it is like a sponge that absorbs everything and imprints it forever inside. How important it is, therefore, that together with mother's milk the little one should also be given the milk of faith! As priests, we must take it very much to heart that the little ones receive correct formation in the faith. Let us not despise them. Let us remember that often Our Lady has not appeared to adults, but to the little ones. This means that they are able to understand and also are able to make sacrifices for God.

Strong faith, instilled in us when we were little or recovered later, must remain like that, that is, solid.

Moreover it must remain strong on both the personal and doctrinal levels. The priest must take good care of his faith, both with appropriate studies and readings (for *fides quae*) and with prayer and penance (for *fides qua*). In Latin we say *nemo dat quod non habet*: no one can give to others what he does not have. So how are we going to give faith if we do not have faith?

It is also helpful, in order to strengthen faith, to put it to the test from time to time. Generally these will be little tests: for example, leaving something undecided in a plan we draw up, to keep our pride from presuming to dominate and determine everything. This means leaving a little empty spot that will be the Lord's business and not mine, to remind me that man proposes but God disposes. Another example is that proposed by a good bishop who is still with us, as part of a course of Spiritual Exercises that he gave. This bishop told the priests who attended the Exercises: "Every now and then, empty your bank account. Take everything there and give it to the poor, or for church repairs, or to buy worthy sacred vestments and vessels. Empty your bank account. In this way you will share the experience of many persons who pin their hopes on the end of the month, on that salary or pension payment. Many thousands of families live like this, and it may be that they have a livelier sense of Providence than do many priests who are carefree in this sense simply because they have a pot of money set aside."

Of course, this is quite a challenge, but that is exactly why we find it so striking. How many faithful have no money, yet we see them happy and serene. They trust

God more than we do. Yes, they have more faith than we do! They certainly have not read as many books as we have, they do not know as many things as we do. Perhaps they know only a few things about the faith, but those few things, they really live.

Let us put our faith to the test a little every now and then. If we do not feel like emptying our bank account because our faith is too small for that, then let us think of something easier. But in the Bible God often puts the faith of his chosen ones to the test, to see if they truly believe in him. Don't the Spiritual Exercises also come down to this? Isn't this a time to lay bare and then test the state of our faith? Isn't it a time to ask God to give us more faith, to increase our faith, as the apostles asked? (*Lk* 17:6.) Of course, the Spiritual Exercises are also this. Do we want to be more zealous priests? Let us ask the Lord to increase our faith, and for our part let us use good means to reach this good end. Lord, increase our faith! (*Lk* 17:6.) Abraham had faith in the Lord and God credited it to him as righteousness (*Gn* 15:6; cf. *Rm* 4:20-25).

To conclude, a little edifying anecdote from the biography of St John Bosco. One day the saint literally had not a thing to put on the table to feed the many young pupils at his oratory. Nor did he have any cash on hand to buy something. The situation was desperate: he would be happy to fast, but what about his boys? He went to the chapel and addressed a heartfelt plea to St Joseph, because St Joseph's task on earth was to provide everything that Jesus and Mary needed. A little while later a gentleman he had never seen before appeared at the gate of the oratory and left a large amount of food to feed the children housed there. St Joseph had struck again!

We learn something very important from this story. St John Bosco was certainly not naive. He had not inaugurated or developed his project without any concern about financial management, on the contrary we know that many of his duties concerned the administration of the newborn institution. But with such a project, unforeseen things can happen, like that day when there was no food at all for the boys. Don Bosco, however, knew that where man cannot foresee, God can provide. He also knew he had not started that project by following a personal plan of his own, but in accordance with the plan God had inspired him with. Don Bosco's work was in reality the work of Jesus. Jesus, therefore, at least in emergencies, had to intervene. And he always did.

Episodes of this kind can be found by the thousands in the lives of the saints. Why? Not because they were supermen, but because they were men of faith. We pray that the Holy Spirit may also give us the simple and solid faith of the saints.

The Priesthood not as "Work" but as a Path of Sanctification for the Priest and the Flock Entrusted to him

Let us return to the theme of faith. Living by faith means living centred in God through Jesus Christ, under the action of the Holy Spirit. The Holy Spirit who dwells in the soul of the priest orders his life in a theocentric and Christocentric way, that is, God and Christ are the centre, the Life of his life. It is very important to reflect on this orientation that the Holy Spirit himself possesses and as a result instils within souls.

In recent Catholic theology, more than in the past, there has been development in pneumatological reflection. Among the many possible examples, we could recall here the three volume work by Yves Congar entitled *I Believe in the Holy Spirit*. Why has pneumatological theological literature developed more in recent decades? There may be many reasons. One segment of theologians realised that Catholic theology seemed less complete than the Orthodox with regard to the Third Person of the Trinity – this is a first reason: a desire to fill a "pneumatological void". There were certainly ecumenical reasons as well. Everyone is aware of the painful split that took place between the Roman and Constantinopolitan Churches, under the patriarch Michael Cerularius in 1054. Several recent studies (see M. Gagliardi, *Il Filioque*, Libreria Editrice Vaticana, 2015) show that the question of the *Filioque* was probably not the real cause of the separation of Constantinople from Rome. This doctrinal reason may have been added later, as the true reasons for the schism lie elsewhere. Leaving aside historiographical theories, it is a fact that for almost a thousand years now the doctrine of the *Filioque* has represented one of the main stumbling blocks that seem to justify the separation of the Orthodox Churches from the Catholic Church. As a result, the theologians of the twentieth century felt a responsibility to deepen study of the doctrine on the Holy Spirit, to see if and how doctrinal misunderstandings could be reduced or even eliminated. So this would be a second reason for the increase in pneumatological attention in the Catholic domain: the new ecumenical sensitivity developed around the time of the Second Vatican Council.

We would also like to mention a third reason, in some way connected with the second. Ecumenism is in fact intended not only for the Orthodox but also for the various Protestant communities. In particular, Catholic theologians have tried to reformulate the theological understanding of grace, taking into account the Protestant approach as well, in which the theme of the subjective experience of salvation is important. For classical Catholic theology, grace was not so much a matter of "feeling" saved as of "being" objectively saved. This also led to the emphasis placed on the sacraments as efficacious and objective signs of grace. But for Luther and the movements he inspired, the theme was instead: "How do *I* find a merciful God?" The emphasis falls on the "I". Luther is a true representative of modernity, with his emphasis on the human subject.

Catholic theologians, therefore, felt a responsibility to reinterpret the theology of grace partly on the basis of this insistence on somehow subjectively perceiving grace. And this dovetails with study of the Holy Spirit, seen as the one who gives us this "experience" of grace. Within the bounds of a course of Spiritual Exercises, we cannot and must not go into theological questions in depth. These brief remarks serve only to indicate some of the reasons why, for several decades now, much more has been said and written about the Third Person of the Trinity than in the past. Nor is it our task in this setting to denounce the problems and critical condition of many new approaches to pneumatology.

Let us dwell only on the positive: of course it is good to study the figure of the Holy Spirit more, so that good theology may help us, as far as possible, to better understand who he is and how he acts, he who is the Third person in God. Here let us leave aside the various problems of recent pneumatology and dwell only on what is good.

So then, various Catholic pneumatologists have pointed out one absolutely true fact to us. The Bible generally does not put the Holy Spirit front and centre. He is clearly revealed in Scripture, but he generally prefers to remain hidden, silent. He acts, this is certain, but does not claim a leading role, although he has one. Except for a single case, the Holy Spirit never speaks in the first person. The only exception is in Acts 13:2 in which the Spirit says: "Set apart for me Barnabas and Saul for the work to which I have called them." In all the other numerous texts in which the Bible mentions the Holy Spirit, he does not speak. He acts, it is true; but he does so in such a way that the emphasis is on the incarnate Son and, through him, the Father. Theologians therefore say that the task of the Holy Spirit, so to speak, is not to draw attention to himself, but rather to convey it to Christ and, through Christ, to the Father. He carries out a Christocentric and theocentric action. The Holy Spirit speaks very little. Indeed, according to the beautiful expression of one Catholic theologian, the Holy Spirit says just one word: "Jesus" (*Jn* 15:26-27; 16:13-15).

These beautiful reflections, based on Scripture, were revisited doctrinally in the most succinct and systematic manner by the declaration *Dominus Iesus*, which confirmed the faith of the Church in many fundamental doctrines, including the fact that the Holy Spirit's action in the world and in the Church is not and could not be alternative to or in competition with the work of Jesus Christ. In other words, the Holy Spirit does not deal with things different from those of Christ, he does not set up parallel ways of salvation, alternatives to the only way that is Jesus Christ. The Holy Spirit, on the contrary, always directs men towards the paschal mystery of Jesus, as was seen back before *Dominus Iesus* in the teaching of the Second Vatican Council. It is utterly mistaken to think that the Holy Spirit constructs parallel or alternative paths of salvation. The Holy Spirit, on the contrary, draws men to the one true way: Jesus Christ.

Within the Church, then, the Holy Spirit infuses souls with the grace of Christ. Not a different grace, but that of the Lord Jesus, which he earned on the cross. For this reason, Vatican II speaks of the "paschal mystery" of Christ (*Gaudium et Spes* 22) with which the Spirit puts men in contact: this is the mystery of the passion, death and resurrection. We are made partakers in this mystery through the work of the Holy Spirit in many ways, but above all through the objectivity of the sacraments.

It is, for example, the action of the Holy Spirit who, in Baptism, washes sins away and grafts men into the Mystical Body of the incarnate Son. The theologians specify that in reality it is the whole Trinity that operates in the world and never just one Person, except in the case of the Incarnation of the Word, when we consider that as regards its final end (i.e., the union of the two natures). Nonetheless, speaking by way of appropriation, we have always said that the Holy Spirit does this. In the same way we recall that, in the Holy Mass, it is the Holy Spirit, invoked over the offerings through the epiclesis, who carries out the transubstantiation of the bread and wine into the Body and Blood of Christ. All this, and much more, the Holy Spirit does in a discreet way, in a silent way, without wanting to appear or be the protagonist. And yet he is, with his divine power.

He is the secret Guest of the souls of the just who are in the state of grace. He is the Principle of the Trinitarian indwelling within us. Catholic theology of the past may have cared less about reflection on the Third Person precisely for this reason: he is supremely discreet and silent, which is by no means to say that he is absent or inert. He works with "the power of silence". That is why one of the visible effects of his action and presence in us is precisely this: whether and to what extent we have the capacity for silence, interior and exterior.

His great discretion, however, should not justify our carelessness towards him. In her Tradition the Church has been attentive in this regard, if not always at the theological level then certainly at the liturgical and devotional level. The solemnity of Pentecost has been part of the liturgical calendar since time immemorial. In addition, the Church has composed magnificent hymns to worship and pray to the Holy Spirit, such as the famous *Veni, Sancte Spiritus* or *Veni, Creator Spiritus*. The saints, moreover, have always cultivated devotion to the Holy Spirit, which is very important. If I may offer a personal recollection, I will mention that in a sense my family and I owe the fact of our being Christian to a religious congregation that is under the patronage of the Third Person: the Spiritan Fathers, who with enormous personal sacrifice evangelised my native land and an important part of Africa.

Here then, in speaking of priestly sanctification, we must recall these elements (although only briefly expounded here) concerning the Spirit of God who is God himself. The sanctification of the priest is, of course, the work of the Holy Spirit. And here we must pay attention. We have said: what does the Spirit do? He leads us to Christ and, through him, to the Father. Therefore, the sanctifying action of the Holy Spirit in us consists in this: he wants to lead priests to Christ and, through Christ, to God the Father. "I am the way, the truth and the life. No one comes to the Father except through me" (*Jn* 14:6). Sanctification is Christocentric and theocentric.

A holy priest, then, is not one who lives without points of reference. His points of reference are Christ and God. The priest is not someone who seeks alternative paths, new paths. In fact, the Spirit does not open paths alternative to the only way. On the contrary, the priest is called to travel with perfection the path that is the Master, Jesus, the Son of God who leads him to see and contemplate the Father's face. "If you have known me, you will also know my Father: from now on you know him and have seen him" (*Jn* 14:7). Again, the priest is sanctified by the Spirit according to the usual way in which this divine Person acts, meaning in an objective and effective way, but silently rather than in a pompous and noisy manner. In other words, as for every other Christian, sanctification for the priest is not a subjective experience of grace, but rather consists of an objective and effective action of the Holy Spirit in him.

This last aspect is of particular relevance. Today even vast sectors of the Catholic Church seem to have been penetrated by a spirituality bearing certain Protestant traits. We say this without prejudice to our separated brethren. It is just an observation. According to Protestant spirituality (although here we cannot distinguish among the many types of Protestantism that exist), we can say that the aspect of "feeling saved" is fundamental. This feeling of one's salvation can then also be declined in very different ways according to the various forms of Protestantism. The spirituality of a classical Lutheran, for example, does not match that of the recent Pentecostal movements. In any case it is like this: for the Protestant it is fundamental to "know" in some way that he is justified. But for us Catholics the most important thing is not "knowing" or "experiencing", but having the elements of moral certainty in order prudently to lay claim to "being" in the grace of God. It is less a question of experience and more one of objectivity. This, at least, according to classical Catholic spirituality.

We were saying that recently sensitivity to the experience of grace has penetrated large parts of the Church. This is noticeable both in practices of spirituality and in the Liturgy. One of the reasons, for example, why so many priests commit liturgical abuses, introducing into the sacred rites things not provided for by the norms of the Church, lies precisely in this: they maintain that the rite, if faithfully observed, would be repetitive and boring. So they conclude that something must be done to personalise it, make it our own, connect it with our feelings. The faithful must feel involved in the liturgical action, they must experience a feeling of joy, perhaps even euphoria, and be in a state of exaltation during the celebration. According to this perspective, such "feeling" would not be possible if one were to respect the rite in the way the Church has established it.

Other examples could be added. One of them concerns moments of silence, both in the Liturgy and in other moments of prayer. In many places one notes a true inability to be silent before the Lord. Psalm 38:10 says, addressing God: "Dumbstricken, I do not open my mouth, because it is you who act." This is a very beautiful phrase, expressing very well the spirit of prayer and adoration. Before the Lord, we do not need to say very many words. Let us recall the famous episode of that peasant from the parish of Ars who spent a long time in church, in front of the tabernacle. One day, the holy Curé asked him how he was spending his time, what he was doing, what he was thinking about, what he was saying to the Lord during his long visits. And the peasant replied, "Nothing, Father. I look at him and he looks at me." That peasant may not have known verse 10 of Psalm 38, but he certainly lived it!

> The Spirit helps us in our weakness; for we do not know how to pray as we ought, but the Spirit himself intercedes for us with sighs too deep for words. And he who searches the hearts of men knows what is

the mind of the Spirit, because the Spirit intercedes for the saints according to the will of God. (*Rm* 8:26-27)

"Dumbstricken, I do not open my mouth, because it is you who act." The Holy Spirit is silent, he hardly ever speaks. One icon of the Holy Spirit is St Joseph, who never speaks in the Gospels; but he certainly acts! The Holy Spirit does not blow the trumpet before him like the Pharisees would when he does something good for us. He does it and that's it. We do not perceive his presence and his action except through the gifts he gives and the fruits he produces. This is how we too learn that true spirituality consists in standing before God in silence, because he is the one who acts.

Let us go back to what we were saying about the lack of a capacity for silence among many priests and faithful today. We know that the rite of Mass approved by Paul VI explicitly provides for moments of sacred silence. But today, how many priests observe these? And this is also true outside the Mass. For example, when Eucharistic adoration is held in the parish, it may be helpful to read some short biblical passages or a work by a saint to foster meditation and contemplation. But often the whole hour of adoration is filled with readings and songs. And in the moments that would otherwise be silent there is still music in the background or even recorded music set up to accompany the silence. But does this musical background truly accompany the silence, or wipe it out? Does it not destroy it?

There is often a tendency towards the sentimental in both the texts that are read and the songs that are sung. Where does this spiritual sentimentalism come from? Probably from the idea we mentioned above: that it is necessary to make sure that, during prayer, we feel the "emotion" of the Holy Spirit. Here, however, there may be a trap lurking. The Spirit of God, in fact, certainly effects "motions" in us. That is, he arouses internal movements of our created spirit, allowing us to perceive a spiritual attraction towards the true, the beautiful, and the good, thereby encouraging our conversion. But the "motions" of the Holy Spirit, although not seldom accompanied by a certain feeling, do not coincide *tout court* with the "emotions".

Above all, one must be careful not to identify a certain perception of the Holy Spirit with sensations artfully produced through prayer techniques or pseudo-liturgical creations. In this case, in fact, man would take the place of God. It would no longer be the Holy Spirit who – as the Lord teaches – blows where he wills. Here the Spirit is supposed to blow where and when we will. He is supposed to put himself at the service of the success of our religious meetings by guaranteeing and ensuring that everyone "feel" satisfied in such circumstances.

But the centuries-old spiritual experience of the saints shows that this is not how things are. The Holy Spirit can certainly give an intimate feeling of peace and joy, and many times he does so. But he does so how, when, and where he wills, that is, when he sees that this is good for us. Many other times the Holy

Spirit can also act in us in the form of desolation, as shown – to mention just two names – by the great Carmelite saints Teresa of Avila and John of the Cross. Not only spiritual joy, but the dark night too is a way in which the Holy Spirit manifests himself and acts.

In short, on his path of holiness the priest is not called to seek sensations, he must not aim to "feel good". Instead, he must follow the spiritual motions that orient him to the good and awaken his missionary zeal for the salvation of souls. And he must do this whether such motions are received in joy or occur in moments of discouragement or humiliation or desolation. Holiness is not a state of mind, but is something objective. It is important to quote in this regard verse 5 of chapter 2 of the Letter to the Philippians. We know that Philippians 2:5-11 contains the famous Christological hymn, which describes the descending and ascending course of Christ, who, though being of divine condition, humbled himself even to the cross and then was exalted in glory. But this hymn is introduced by St Paul as follows: "Have in yourselves the same sentiments as Christ Jesus". This is how the Italian Bible translates it. But we must understand what these "sentiments" of Jesus are. In the original Greek, St Paul does not use a noun, but a verb: *phronéite*. The term *phronéin* does not indicate superficial and fleeting sentiments, but rather thought and the action that follows from it. So St Paul says to the Philippians (and to all of us): act in a way consistent with right thinking, as did Christ, who, though being God, humbled himself, etc. These are the "sentiments" of Christ! Right thinking and right action. These are objective things, not moods. It is sad to see how in some (indeed, in many) seminaries for decades now, future priests have been taught a subjective and sentimental way of praying. The seminary should look more like a military academy where young cadets are tempered for future battles than a school of sentimental pseudo-psychological techniques. So let us recover a sound vision of holiness, which also implies the manliness proper to the minister of God.

PART II

This morning's last remark concerned the manliness of the priest. Among the many aspects this involves, there is also that typical aspect of masculine psychology which consists in taking charge of a family and providing for it. This brings back up again the image of St Joseph, who for us priests is always a great inspiration. He was most chaste, as we must also be, although the Western world has a satanic plan to destroy our priestly chastity. He lived a true marriage with Mary, in perfect continence. Still, he was a true husband and a true father. That is, as a real man, he took on his responsibilities. Although he was not Jesus's natural father, he assumed paternal responsibility for Christ the moment he accepted the vocation revealed to him by the angel. Moreover, even before these events he had betrothed himself to Mary. Not even in the face of the extraordinary novelty of the Incarnation of the Word in her did St Joseph break his vow. He took with him his betrothed, and also that Child whom she was now carrying in her virginal womb through the work of the Holy Spirit, and he took care of them until his death.

How can we not see in this an example for the priest? The priest, as we were saying, is called to perfect continence, like St Joseph. And like him, as the true man he is, the priest must take on his responsibilities for his bride and children. The priest's bride is the Church. His children are the faithful. The priest's path to holiness is not an isolated path. He travels the paths of holiness together with his bride and his children.

It is beautiful and important to emphasise both the full manliness and the spousal and paternal character of every priest. We know that only men (*viri*) can be ordained, and that this is according to the will of Christ, a will that no one can change. It is also known that in the Latin Church celibacy is an integral part of the vocation to the priesthood. It is true that this is not usually said to be a matter of divine law, but a decision of the Church and therefore a discipline that could be changed. But it is also true that such a change – which in itself would not directly go against doctrine – would represent a serious impoverishment of the established discipline that, according to the Council of Elvira (305) and the Council of Carthage (390), the Church received directly from the apostles. And this is not simply a matter of discipline, but of spirituality, in the strongest sense of the word. There are very serious studies, on the historical and dogmatic level, that affirm that – although celibacy in itself is a discipline that

developed in the Church over time – the continence
of the clergy goes back to the beginning, to Jesus and
the apostles themselves.[1]

We know that at least some of the apostles were
married, therefore celibacy in the strict sense is not
a *conditio sine qua non* for the priesthood. And in fact
priests of the Eastern rite can be chosen from among
married men. But what is often not remembered is that
the custom of the Eastern Churches is that at least on
the day before celebrating the Divine Liturgy (that is,
the Eucharist) the married priest should not unite with
his wife. Even among the Eastern Churches, therefore,
this memory of priestly continence remains, albeit in an
intermittent form. On the other hand, the Latin Church
has long considered it better that priestly continence be
perfect. Hence the ecclesiastical law of celibacy, the aim
of which is precisely the stability of continence. To sum
it up, if it is true that celibacy in itself is an ecclesiastical
law, continence, on the other hand, seems to have been
linked to priestly ministry since the time of the apostles.
Is it not therefore better to observe this continence in
a perfect way, rather than in a discontinuous way? St
Peter – who was married – said to Jesus, "Behold, we

---

[1] "One could argue that the Christian East has always been familiar with this
situation and that it poses no problem. That is false. At a late date, the Christian
East allowed married men who had become priests to have sexual relations
with their spouses. This discipline was introduced at the council in Trullo in
691. The novelty appeared as the result of an error in transcribing the canons
of the council that had been held in 390 in Carthage. The major innovation
of this seventh-century council, moreover, is not the disappearance of priestly
continence but the limitation of it to the periods preceding the celebration
of the Holy Mysteries. The ontological bond between priestly ministry and
continence is still established and perceived." (Robert Sarah, *From the Depths of
Our Hearts*, Ignatius Press, San Francisco 2020, pp. 79-80.)

have left everything and followed you" (*Mt* 19:27). The apostle could not have spoken this way if he had stayed home with his wife. Perfect continence is implied in this "everything" to which St Peter refers. Otherwise, it would have been only leaving "a part", or "at certain times and not others".

As is well known, the pastoral letters of the New Testament describe the bishop as "man of one wife", in Latin *unius uxoris vir*. On this formula as well there are various interpretations by exegetes and theologians, which we must not dwell on here (*1 Tm* 3:2; 3:12 on deacons). Even assuming that at first bishops were married and therefore the formula, on the literal level, would refer to the fact that a bishop could not be chosen from among the divorced and "remarried", on the level of spiritual interpretation the passage reveals truly exceptional potential. A celibate priest must also be *unius uxoris vir*, that is, married to just one woman, and this woman is the Church, to whom he must be faithful his entire life. Thus the priest is a true *vir ecclesiasticus*, a man of the Church, or a man of the Church and for the Church, totally devoted to her, just as every married man must dedicate all his care, his whole life long, to his sole legitimate wife.

Here again we revisit this fine point about the priest's manliness. He must be a real man and therefore also a strong man, a man with broad shoulders, capable of bearing "the burden of the day [that is, of life] and the heat [that is, difficulties]", as we read in the Gospel parable (cf. *Mt* 20:12). It is very sad to see certain priests who, on the contrary, show a certain unmanly weakness in their traits. Of course, manliness does not mean coarseness, discourtesy, aggression. Indeed, it is aptly said that "calmness is the virtue of the strong". Far less does manliness mean vulgarity in speaking, as – alas! – is sometimes found on the lips of certain priests who even allow themselves to use double meanings of a sexual nature when they talk to people, or readily resort to the use of bad words and vulgarity. Doing this is not part of being a real man, but only of being inappropriate and rude, at the same time also giving scandal. May it never happen that vulgarity or triviality be found in our speech! Not even when we socialise with our faithful, particularly the young. Being among people we must be – as Chrysostom says – splendid like the sun. Even when spending time among young people, we must always represent Christ in their midst, and never just want to be one friend among the rest. Friends, yes; but with distinction. Love and kindness towards all, but avoiding excessive familiarity. A father who did not act as a father but as a friend to his children, placing himself on the same level as them, would be harming his children. It is right to be loving; it is wrong not to be authoritative. A father, in addition to giving love, must also be able moderately to demand the respect due to his role. And this too is love, because this is good for children, it educates them, brings them up well, that is, with order. An excessive familiarity of the priest with the faithful is always harmful. This is not to say that he should be cold and aloof. A father, yes.

The priest, a true, strong and loving man, is therefore a husband and father. The masculine psychology of the priest fits well with the spousal relationship with the Woman-Church. There exists a spirituality of mystical marriage with the Bridegroom Jesus Christ. Generally speaking, this profound spirituality is more suited to the female psyche than to the male. A consecrated woman will find herself more at ease than a priest in this respect, unless the priest receives special illumination from God, calling him to be sanctified by this path. It is possible, but it seems that these cases are rare. What seems more pertinent to priestly spirituality is the spousal relationship with the Woman, that is, with the Church. The priest has married the Church. He has to think about her night and day. He must be in love with the Church. Love for the Church will lead him to sacrifice himself willingly for her, for her growth and support, for the beautiful shining forth of her holiness.

The priest in love will also always want to defend the Church from enemy attacks. This too is normal for those who love. In the past, seminaries taught apologetics. For several decades this has not been taught anymore, because – we are told – it is a mere intellectual exercise and, moreover, it is a non-dialogical attitude. Although one must always beware of rationalism (which, however, can also be present in the more recent theological approaches that have supplanted previous ones), and despite the fact that reasonable dialogue is in itself a good thing, it must be said that apologetics, if developed well, is useful and necessary. We must not be naive. In addition to people who sincerely want to dialogue with Christians, there will always be others who will instead aim to overthrow and destroy Christianity. St Peter tells us that we must always be ready to give a reason (*logos*) for the hope that is in us (cf. *1 P* 3:15). The apostle adds that this must be done with gentleness and respect. But it must be done! And the content of this action is not gentleness and respect which, if it is anything, is the method. The content is the *Logos*. Apologetics arises from here, from the *Logos*, just as all of theology does. Apologetics, then, is an act of love: for God, for Christ, for the Church. Whoever loves defends the beloved against unjust attack. This was the exhortation Paul VI gave us in the Angelus of 19th March 1970. Following in the footsteps of St Joseph, we too must defend the Church, faithfully guard the Doctrine of Christ, protect it from its enemies:

The mission that he [St Joseph] carried out in the Gospel, on behalf of Mary and Jesus in the historical context of the Incarnation, a mission of protection, defence, safekeeping, sustenance, we must hope and implore that the humble, great saint may continue this for the benefit of the Church, which is the Mystical Body of Christ; it is Christ who lives in humanity and continues the work of redemption throughout history. As in the Gospel of the Lord's childhood, the Church needs to be defended and kept intact in the school of Nazareth, poor, hard-working, but lively and always attentive and at the ready for her messianic vocation. She needs protection in order to be unharmed and to operate in the world; and today we can see how great this need is; therefore we will invoke the patronage of St Joseph for the troubled, threatened, suspected, and rejected Church. But it is not enough for us to invoke: we must imitate. And that Christ should have wanted to be protected by a simple craftsman, in the humble abode of family life, teaches us that everyone can likewise protect Christ in the realm of the home and in the world of work, culture, politics and commercial affairs, science and technology. It also persuades us that we all must do so, since we are all capable of professing, defending, and affirming the Christian name in our home and in the exercise of our work. St Joseph's mission has become our own: to guard and raise Christ in us and around us.

Unfortunately, alongside many good priests there are others who instead are themselves the first to attack or deride their spouse, the Church. What would we think of a man who, when he is in the pub with his friends, does nothing but malign his wife? Look, these priests who attack the Church, often even on television, are like such men. While they think they are making themselves look good, gaining the approval of those who listen to them, in reality – speaking ill of the Church – they end up putting themselves in a very bad light. They may receive applause, acclamation, and more talk show invitations. But deep in their hearts, those who hear them talk this way despise them. Yes, even those who invite them to speak on television invite them because they are useful puppets in the hands of those who run show business. They invite them, but secretly despise them. They are "useful idiots", not to mention "useful traitors" to their own ecclesial blood. Could we ever imagine St Joseph speaking a crooked word about Mary? Rather than do this he would have cut out his tongue! That is what we priests must also do: never mock the Church in public! Our being baptised makes her our mother; our being priests makes her our beloved bride.

And then there are the children. We know well, also from experience, that the sanctification of the priest consists, day by day, in taking care – because we are "curates" – of our beloved children in Christ. Not so long ago there was this beautiful custom: all the faithful called their priest "father", and the priest often addressed them, for example when beginning the homily, by calling them children. Today, too often, the faithful call the priest directly by his name. This is a deviation typical of our time, as is addressing everyone informally, even the pope! In Africa, even today, children never call mum or dad by their names. It may seem strange, but it's not. In several episodes in the Bible we see angels, heavenly messengers, refusing to reveal their names. In fact, the use of the name indicates an intimacy reserved for a few. Of course, today it is unthinkable, at least in the West, that a priest should not be known by his name. But some signs of respect must be preserved. For example, it is not good for everyone to address the priest informally. Close friends, of course, may do so. But not all the faithful. Also not good is the habit of calling him only by his name, without prefacing "Father".

One priest told this story: when he was a seminarian, the bishop sent him on a pastoral internship to a parish where he remained for a few years. He would go there at the weekend and do what he could to give the priest a hand. In those years, the people of the parish obviously knew him as a seminarian and called him by the informal "tu", used his first name, which is understandable, partly on account of his youth. When he was ordained a deacon, the elderly priest told all the parishioners that, from that day on, everyone had to add "Don" before that young man's name. At first some turned up their noses, and even the new deacon himself told the priest it was not necessary. But the priest, who often turned a blind eye to many things, was adamant on this point. He said to the young new deacon, "From today on you are no longer just a member of the faithful; you are a minister of God and of the Church." And every time one of the faithful, by mistake, addressed the deacon without the "Don", the priest would scold them. He did so for many months, until the whole parish learned to call the new minister of God "Don". Telling the story years later, the deacon, then a priest, said, "At first I did not understand why the priest insisted so much; it seemed excessive to me. I was even in favour of their continuing to call me just by my name. But later, over the years, I understood. The priest was right and today I thank him for teaching me and the others this lesson."

This is just a simple anecdote to indicate a reality that is much deeper: in the midst of Christ's flock, once ordained, we no longer represent ourselves, but him. Putting "Father" in front of a name is not a worldly honour, but is intended concretely to indicate this fundamental truth. In this way the faithful will implicitly remember who we are: ministers of God and of the Church. But not only them: we will remember too! To hear ourselves called "Father", even politely to insist on being so addressed, does not represent – let us repeat – vanity or striving for worldly honour. On the contrary, it is a call to responsibility. This is also true outside the priesthood. A lawyer once said, "I am against the abolition of titles." He was referring to the fact that often in contemporary society, even in formal relationships, titles such as "engineer", "professor", and the like are no longer used, but one is immediately on a first-name basis. For example, someone goes to the office of a sixty-year-old engineer. He doesn't introduce himself by saying, "Pleased to meet you, Engineer Bianchi." He says, "Pleased to meet you, Giulio." And if anyone calls him by his proper title, he replies, "Call me Giulio, not 'Engineer'; and use 'tu', because 'lei' makes me feel old." So that lawyer said, "I am against the abolition of titles, because titles are not only honorific. They certainly indicate a dignity, a position in society. But the reason why the very people who hold them today tend to abandon them is because they don't want to take on the responsibilities that the title entails."

We can also apply this observation to the question of priestly attire. How many priests do not wear the proper attire of their state! And why not? One of the justifications offered most frequently is that, by dressing like everyone else, they can blend into society and be accepted by people and, in this way, get closer to them. On this we need to make a few brief reflections, because there are some historical cases that can be invoked. Well known, for example, is the case of the Jesuit missionary Matteo Ricci, who after he arrived in China discarded his religious attire and dressed like a Mandarin, a public official, which got him welcomed at the court of the emperor. There, however, Ricci was dealing with matters that were not purely religious. He was trying to fit into a closed society, hoping that after doing so he could open it to evangelisation. Another case, well known to historians but a bit less so to the general public, is that of another Jesuit, Roberto de Nobili, a missionary in India. He too exchanged religious attire for that of a noble Indian caste, to facilitate social acceptance. But de Nobili dedicated himself to direct evangelisation, also translating the catechism and prayer books into Tamil. His mission met with some success in terms of conversions, although he never reached the astronomical numbers of baptised persons obtained by St Francis Xavier, who instead always wore Jesuit attire.

We cite these examples to propose a reflection: when priests do not wear the attire proper to them, are we sure that here, in the West of the twenty-first century, we are in conditions like those of China or India in centuries gone by? Secondly: the priest who does not dress as a priest, what is he suggesting by getting closer to people? To evangelise them in order to bring them to Christ, or to blend in with the masses? We must note that many of those priests, who claim dressing in this way keeps people from resisting their approach, do not go on to carry out a mission of evangelisation with such people.

In reality, exactly because our society is certainly secularised but still bears strong traces of the Christian centuries, people need the priest to be among them as a priest; and this includes being visible as such. In some cases this may inconvenience the priest, but that is part of our mission. Among all social categories, it is only some priests today who think they can do their duty without wearing the uniform. Policemen, magistrates, lawyers, academic authorities...all have kept the traditional attire of their state. And they are right to keep it! Yet in our case it is not just a uniform to be used only when on duty. Or perhaps it is, because our duty never ends! This is why we must always dress as priests. It is clear that there may be particular situations in which one is not strictly obliged: taking exercise, or hiking in the mountains...but beyond cases like these, we should always be recognisable as fathers to our children and, to non-Catholics, as ministers of God and of the Catholic Church. This is not formalism, it is a matter of substance.

The priest's holiness is marked by constant availability to his children. A father is not a father by the hour. A father is always a father. There are some places in the world where the priest decides to hear confessions only on Saturdays for half an hour. If someone comes to the rectory during the week, even if the priest has nothing to do at that moment, he refuses: "Here you can go to confession only on Saturdays between five and five-thirty." What father talks like this? In the Gospel Jesus says, "If you then, who are evil, know how to give good things to your children..." (*Lk* 11:13). Even bad men, criminals, mobsters, when it comes to their children, they make themselves available. To our chagrin we must say that some priests do not act like fathers and are worse than bad men. Because even the bad ones know how to give good things to their children when they ask them! We must certainly moderate the excessive or untimely demands of our children, but we must be fathers, that is, available and generous. With the priest, one act of availability is worth more than a thousand homilies.

Let us ask Mary, Mother of priests, to teach us to be true fathers for our children and true husbands for the Church.

The Dignity of the Liturgy as a Way of Sanctification for the Priest: Laziness in the Liturgy is a Spiritual Disease for the Priest

PART I

Yesterday we spoke of the priest's path to holiness, referring to the action of the sanctifying Spirit in his soul. We recalled that the Holy Spirit leads the priest to be husband of the Church and father of the faithful. As a result, we have understood that the priesthood is not a job like any other, a job on the clock. It is a vocation and a mission that lasts a lifetime and extends to all of existence, day and night, without delimited shifts and schedules. The priest does not simply *act* as minister of God; he *is* minister of God and representative of Christ.

We also emphasised yesterday that the Holy Spirit carries out his action in a silent and discreet way, orientating the soul towards Christ and towards God. Sanctification, therefore, is produced in the priest by the theocentric and Christocentric orientation of his entire life. These two orientations can be identified in a single fundamental orientation of our life, which is the Christological-Trinitarian one. Theocentrism and Christocentrism are not two opposite orientations, but two converging lines of a single directionality, impressed on our soul by the Trinitarian Third Person.

To understand this concentricity of theocentric and Christocentric orientation, it seems useful to recall the vision of St John in chapter 7 of Revelation. The seer contemplates the throne of God, in front of which are the angels and the hosts of the one hundred and forty-four thousand in adoration, from every tribe of the children of Israel (verse 4). Verse 9 says, "All stood before the throne and before the Lamb, clothed in white garments, with palm branches in their hands". The next verse then states, "And they cried aloud: 'Salvation belongs to our God, seated on the throne, and to the Lamb.'" The text as presented could lead one to think that God and the Lamb are in two different places: God seated on the throne and the Lamb perhaps beside the throne itself. But this is not the case. In fact, two chapters earlier, in chapter 5, St John had reported an important detail of his celestial vision: the Lamb is not beside but on the throne, together with the elder, that is, with God. In verse 6 of chapter 5, the apostle writes: "I saw, in the middle of the throne, surrounded by the four living beings and the elders, a Lamb, standing as if slain". So the Lamb is standing, a sign that he is alive, but at the same time he is "as if slain". A lamb, when slain or slaughtered, is dead and does not stand upright. This Lamb, in spite of appearing slain, stands upright.

This is a clear reference to Christ, who died and rose again. Jesus in heaven is alive forever, he stands up. But he continues for all eternity to bear the marks of his glorious Passion. Therefore he is also "as if slain".

Well then, according to St John, the glorified Christ, who bears the stigmata of the Passion, is not beside the throne of God but at its centre. "I saw, in the middle of the throne, [...] a Lamb", says the seer. Thanks to this clarification of chapter 5, the vision of chapter 7 also becomes clearer. When the angels and the one hundred and forty-four thousand prostrate themselves in adoration towards the throne, they, through a single prostration, a single act of worship, are worshipping both the elder who sits on the throne, God, and the Lamb, Christ, who stands in the middle of the throne. We can make a mental contemplation of this image, thinking of the heavenly throne where God the Father sits and, on his knees, the Lamb who stands as if slain.

This identification of the theological and Christological mystery becomes even clearer in chapter 21 of Revelation. There, he who sits on the throne says, "I am the Alpha and the Omega, the Beginning and the End. To him who is thirsty I will give freely to drink from the fountain of the water of life" (verse 6). Now, in chapter 1 verse 8 of Revelation, the characterisation as Alpha and Omega was attributed to Christ, not to the Father, and so it seems to be also in Revelation 22:13. Moreover, in the Gospel of John, Christ says of himself that he will satisfy forever those who thirst for eternal life (cf. *Jn* 4:14; 6:35). Thus, two statements that in the Johannine corpus concern Christ are, in chapter 21 of

Revelation, attributed to himself by the One who sits on the throne, God. Thus the identification between theological mystery and Christological mystery becomes even more apparent. We know well and believe that, as Persons, the Father and the Son are distinct. But we are monotheists, we believe in one God and this God is called Trinity. For this reason, the Father can attribute to himself – because they are truly his – the non-personal characteristics of the Son, such as being the Beginning and End of everything, as well as being he who quenches the thirst of souls. The Holy Spirit too, if he wanted to speak in the first person, could say the same things about himself, because – as St Anselm teaches – in God everything is one, except where there is an opposition of relationship, that is, except where the incommunicable personality of each Trinitarian Person distinguishes itself. According to this principle, in God everything is common to the Three except for the personal features of each divine hypostasis. Since being the Beginning and End of everything is not a personal feature of the Son, the Father and the Spirit are also the Beginning and End, Alpha and Omega, because it is God (the Trinity) who is so.

Finally, in the great vision of Revelation we also find the Holy Spirit. In verse 1 of chapter 22 we read: "And then he showed me a river of living water, clear as crystal, which flowed from the throne of God and of the Lamb". The *Catechism of the Catholic Church* in paragraph 1137 teaches that this image of the river that flows from the throne of God and of the Lamb is one of the most beautiful images of the Holy Spirit:

74

The book of Revelation of St John, read in the Church's Liturgy, first reveals to us, "A throne stood in heaven, with one seated on the throne": "the Lord God." It then shows the Lamb, "standing, as though it had been slain": Christ crucified and risen, the one high priest of the true sanctuary, the same one "who offers and is offered, who gives and is given." Finally it presents "the river of the water of life…flowing from the throne of God and of the Lamb," one of most beautiful symbols of the Holy Spirit. (*CCC* 1137)

Incidentally, this verse contains two interesting aspects. The first is that we explicitly find the expression "the throne of God and of the Lamb", which sets a definitive seal on what we have said so far: Father and Son are one mystery, albeit in mutual personal distinction, and therefore the one throne belongs to both. Secondly, we note that this verse can be considered one of the scriptural passages in which the dogma of the *Filioque* is revealed. *Spiritum Sanctum, Dominum et vivificantem, qui ex Patre Filioque procedit. Qui cum Patre et Filio simul adoratur et conglorificatur.* It is said in fact that the river, meaning the Holy Spirit, springs from the throne of the Father and the Son, flowing from the throne of both.

But here we want to focus our attention on the most central aspect of the image: the river gushing from the throne. Let us again use the contemplative imagination: we see the throne with the venerable Ancient and, on his knees, the Lamb upright and slain. The eye of the beholder sees these Two above all. But in a more discreet, less conspicuous way, there is also a Third who occupies the throne: it is that river which flows from the throne of the Father and of the Son. The Holy Spirit is less noticeable, but he is there. And the throne is also his. Thus the whole Trinity is the one God who sits on the throne of divine majesty.

The divine River flows and enters the world to do its work. We would also like to note another detail. The Lamb is said, in the past tense, to have been slain. His present is to remain alive, standing on the throne, while his past is to have come into the world to die for us. For the Holy Spirit, however, we have the present tense: the river flows. This present certainly indicates the eternal present of God. But perhaps we can see something more: the Word acted in the economy of salvation when he came to earth to sacrifice himself for sinners – and of these sinners we are the first. The Spirit in the present, meaning in every era of history, continues to flow in the economy, to lead men and women to Christ and, through Christ, to God the Father.

In this sense the image of the river has further implications. If we are in a valley and we see a river coming down from the mountains, to find the source we will have to retrace the river's path. There we will find pure water, the pristine water of the spring. In the "valley of tears" (as the Salve Regina calls it) that is this life, flows the river of the Holy Spirit. His presence and action arouse in men the desire for pure water, water that does not slake thirst for only a few moments, but extinguishes thirst forever. The man who wanted to go farther down the valley, to enjoy the entertainments and worldly pleasures of the earthly city, the man who certainly finds it easier to go down than to go up, now – under the attraction of the Spirit – feels something new. He converts, that is, he turns around and changes direction. Now he is prepared for the effort of the climb, because he has understood that the water he will find is worth the effort. The entertainments, sinful or not, of the earthly city no longer interest him as they did before. He knows that even if he obtains them, they will not be able to quench his thirst forever. So he sets out and goes in search of the spring. When he gets there, he finds the throne of God and of the Lamb, from which flows the divine River, the Holy Spirit: that same river which, during his life, attracted and convinced him to follow the path of sanctification.

All these thoughts lead us to consider the role, fundamental to say the least, that the Liturgy has in priestly life. In his extraordinary liturgical encyclical *Mediator Dei*, Pope Pius XII wrote that man's fundamental duty is to orient himself towards God. St Augustine, at the end of his liturgical sermons, used to say to the faithful: *conversi ad Dominum*, "turn to the Lord". The great bishop of Hippo, approaching the end of the Liturgy of the Word with the conclusion of the homily, was preparing to go up to the altar of the Sacrifice. That is why he said, "And now, let us turn to the Lord!" This facing, this turning, was indicated with the Latin verb *convertere*. Strictly speaking the verb means "to turn around" in the physical sense. Of course, the figurative meaning "to change one's life" is also included. Therefore, *conversi ad Dominum* never means just one thing, but always implies two aspects. It is necessary physically to turn to the Lord in order to celebrate the divine Sacrifice of the Mass; and one must also turn around figuratively, that is, one must convert more and more to Christ.

These two aspects of the same word have often been contrasted in the recent mentality, while instead they should always go together, being inseparable according to the Church's thinking. Augustine himself, in one of his sermons, says that it is not enough to turn only physically to the Lord, because all in all that is easy. One must turn both physically and spiritually. Take note here. St Augustine does not say, "It is useless to turn around physically; turn only inwardly." No! He does not oppose these aspects, and says, "Do both!" It is a lesson of great relevance.

In the great battle unleashed in recent times around the Liturgy, this orientation of liturgical action has perhaps been one of the most debated topics. We are in a course of Spiritual Exercises and do not want to enter into this debate in this context. At this moment we are only interested in the implications of the question for the spiritual life of priests. Therefore, without going into many details and clarifications here, we can limit ourselves to noting that two forms of extremism are possible: cherishing liturgical rituals including physical orientation towards the Lord without caring likewise about interior conversion, or the other extreme of striving to live in God's grace but disregarding the importance of liturgical signs in the spiritual life.

We must understand that liturgical signs are a very important aid in spiritual life. They teach and support. They express truths and help us live in keeping with these. Eliminating or even just diminishing the signs in the conviction that interior conversion alone is enough is a fatal mistake, which very often also damages the path of conversion itself. On the other hand, taking good care of the liturgical signs but in a purely aesthetic way, and thereby depriving them of their function as a spur for the moral and spiritual life, is equally mistaken. Man is made up of both soul and body. Therefore we need to turn to the Lord both internally and externally, both physically and spiritually.

The Liturgy represents an extraordinary help in our conversion and sanctification, for two fundamental reasons, linked to the twofold dimension of divine worship as the work of both God and the Church. Insofar as it is the work of God, *operatio Dei*, the sanctifying Spirit acts in the Liturgy. He is the great divine Orientator. He is the River that flows in the Liturgy to direct us towards the eschatological throne. Insofar as it is the work of the Church, *operatio Ecclesiae*, the Liturgy directs us towards God and towards Christ through the gestures and rites established, in her goodness, by mother Church. The Council of Trent, in fact, recalls that the Church has established liturgical rites because she is a loving mother who knows her children's difficulties and wants to help them. Men, Trent recalls, find great difficulty in orienting themselves and rising to the contemplation of eternal realities. For this reason the Church, as a helpful mother, institutes liturgical rites as aids to the soul's elevation towards the contemplation of eternal things. Naturally, in this liturgical institution established by the Church there is also the inspiring action of the Trinitarian Third Person: if not in every single detail and in all particular decisions, certainly as a whole.

Therefore, in the Liturgy too the Holy Spirit is the secret Guest and Inhabitant. He stays silent, but he acts. The most attentive will notice the faint murmur of his voice, like the quiet gurgling of a mountain stream. It is a voice difficult to make out if one is not accustomed to keeping inward and outward silence. The Liturgy, therefore, in addition to being an experience of gestures, rites, and prayers, should always be a school of silence as well: of being silent in order to hear the faint voice of the Holy Spirit. This is why Romano Guardini said, "Indeed, great things happen in silence, not in the noise and pomp of external events, but in the clarity of the inner vision". For Romano Guardini, silence is so fundamental above all in the Liturgy that he said, "If one should ask me where the Liturgy begins, I would reply: by learning silence; without silence everything lacks seriousness and remains empty."

In the Liturgy, the Spirit exercises his main function, which is also in general the end of every grace that is granted to man: to orientate the human being in a theocentric and Christocentric way. The Liturgy is this: to restore primacy to God and worship him on bended knee. An anthropocentric Liturgy, or even an ecclesiocentric one, would be an uncentred Liturgy. The task of divine worship is to reproduce on earth the heavenly Liturgy of the angels and saints. The pilgrim Church imitates the Church triumphant. Now, the Church triumphant is entirely and always turned towards the Lord and not towards itself. The Book of Revelation is a clear attestation of this. Therefore, our Liturgy of the pilgrim or militant Church should also be not a distracting Liturgy, but an attracting Liturgy. The pull of the Spirit is towards God and towards the Lamb. The Holy Spirit does not distract, does not draw our attention to other objects or other purposes.

The worthy and holy celebration of divine worship, with its various elements of *ars celebrandi* and *actuosa participatio*, is a school of theocentric and Christocentric attraction. Therefore the Liturgy is a school of holiness. Because being holy essentially means this: living life while constantly looking to eternity, to our final destiny, that is, to God and to Christ. Holiness is relativising the present in view of the eternal future. It is ordering all things to the goal of reaching the heavenly homeland. Every day the priest can strengthen himself on his path of holiness if he truly celebrates the Liturgy well. Truly celebrating well means celebrating as the Church commands and with all one's heart.

PART II

From what has been said this morning it is clear that the celebration of the Liturgy is the central moment of a priest's day, as well as an essential element of his sanctification. A first clarification to be made, as trivial as it may seem, is that the Liturgy does not consist of the Eucharistic celebration alone, although this does represent the apex of the Church's worship. Let us not forget that Liturgy is also the Divine Office, also commonly called the breviary, not by chance rechristened by Paul VI as Liturgy of the Hours, to manifest the fully liturgical character of this prayer.

When the priest prays the breviary, he is not carrying out a private action. Even if we recite it privately, in our room or in the chapel, even if we are alone, we are not really alone. And not simply because, as Benedict XVI recalled, "those who believe are never alone." There is another reason. Whoever prays the breviary is celebrating the Liturgy of the Hours, that is, presiding over a true liturgical act. If this is done in public, as a community, it is also appropriate to put on the designated liturgical vestments. We do not do this when we pray the breviary in solitude. However, even in this case we are celebrating a true liturgical act; so, in that moment, we represent in ourselves the whole Church. With a beautiful phrase from St Augustine, taken up by Pius XII, we have to remember that in reciting the breviary we must recognise our voices in that of Christ, and his voice in ours. In fact, as St John Paul II recalled, echoing the Church Fathers, when the psalms are proclaimed in the Church it is above all Christ himself who recites them, through the mouth of his Bride. Faithful to the apostolic exhortations to "pray without ceasing", "the divine office is devised so that the whole course of the day and night is made holy by the praises of God" (*Sacrosantum Concilium* 84).

Celebrated "in the form approved" by the Church, the Liturgy of the Hours "is the very prayer which Christ himself, together with his body, addresses to the Father" (ibid. 84).

This is a point of meditation and contemplation for our personal prayer that is presented to us now, but it will remain so even once the Spiritual Exercises are over. Let's really think about this, dear brother priests: every time we recite the psalms of the breviary, Christ speaks through our mouth and, at the same time, our voice enters into the voice of the High Priest Jesus Christ. I advise you to pause often, in the months and years to come, to meditate on this truth, which appears simple but is very profound, because it speaks of the total identification with Christ that the Liturgy of the Hours helps to realise. In this official prayer of the Church, it becomes really visible that this is the Lord's Bride and Mystical Body: one with him. The Body speaks and praises through the mouth, which is found in the Head. The same is true of the Church with regard to Christ. And in the Liturgy of the Hours we are only the visible mouth; the invisible and more important one is the mouth of Jesus who intercedes before the Father for us sinners. So to a certain extent, although it does not measure up to the perfection of the Eucharistic Sacrifice, the breviary also has the value of expiatory prayer. Being, then, the voice of the Bride speaking to her Spouse, the Liturgy of the Hours also has the power, so to speak, to move the priestly Heart of Christ, which will not deny the necessary graces to the children who cry out to him *"die noctuque orantes"*.

Then since we are the mouth of the Lord when we pray the Liturgy of the Hours, we must not rush, because we are representing Christ who prays to the Father. Now Christ never rushes, he speaks unhurriedly with the Father. The Prayer of the Hours is the long, loving and intimate conversation between the Bridegroom and the Bride, an encounter of great intimacy. So let us always pray the Liturgy of the Hours with faith, love, calm, and recollection. Those who love each other are in no hurry to separate, because love is never in a hurry! "*Caritas patiens est…omnia suffert, omnia credit, omnia sperat, omnia sustinet*" (*1 Co* 13:4, 7).

Then we have the Liturgy of the other six sacraments, in addition to the Mass. These are also part of the integral public worship of the Catholic Church, addressed to the Holy Trinity in a theocentric and Christocentric way. We priests must make every effort to celebrate all the sacraments well. Sometimes this can be difficult in human terms, as when we spend several hours straight hearing confessions. In cases like this, it is understandable that weariness can set in, and along with it a bit of sloppiness in celebrating the sacrament. But above all, never take your phone into the confessional! Never. Because you are carrying out a liturgical act, an act of faith. You are with God and in the place of God. So during these Spiritual Exercises we must strengthen our faith. How? By making our contemplative gaze firmer. Let us accumulate spiritual energy to be used throughout the year, until the next Exercises. Energy that we must expend when we sit in the confessional or celebrate other sacraments. Let us do it right, with care!

Let us first thoroughly prepare all that is necessary, so that the celebration may not disturbed by unforeseen events, for example if something necessary for the rite were to be missing. Let us use liturgical vestments and sacred linens in good condition, stored and laundered well. Let us not mumble the prayers or hasten the rites. While not being pointlessly slow or stodgy, let us make every gesture and say every word with sober solemnity and with the time it takes. There is no need to add other things, of our own invention, if we celebrate the rite well.

Let us do likewise with the sacramentals. A seminarian was once standing outside the lower basilica in Lourdes. While he was waiting for someone, he saw a priest come out in an alb and stole. This priest was a bit impatient, or at least he was in a bit of a hurry because baptisms were about to be celebrated in the basilica but one of the families had not yet arrived. So he was looking anxiously across the *esplanade* to see if the delayed family was coming. Two pilgrims who had just bought Lourdes candles to take home in memory of their pilgrimage saw him in his priestly vestments and came up to him. They kindly asked the priest to bless the candles, and the priest, continuing to look across the *esplanade*, without even saying a prayer, made a very hasty sign of the cross more or less in the direction of the candles, although rather than a sign of the cross it almost looked as if he was shooing flies. He realised he had done wrong, and tried to fix it somehow. What he did was simply to touch the candles with his hand and then kiss his own hand, the one he had briefly touched to the candles, as if to say with that gesture: "Don't worry, the candles are blessed." It is difficult to describe the expression on the face of those two pilgrims, husband and wife, who were preparing to return home and, full of enthusiasm, had approached that minister of God. What would it have cost to have given a little extra attention? Maybe ask where they were from, say a good word, give a little encouragement. And then pray a Hail Mary or an Our Father, and give a blessing properly. That priest would have spent one, at most two minutes, but the seed he could have sown through that little bit of attention could have borne great fruit and would certainly have avoided giving great disappointment and scandal.

I repeat, sometimes in all of us fatigue or other thoughts can prevail. Let us not be too critical of that poor hasty priest! But the seminarian who witnessed that scene, who today is a priest, remembers it clearly, even a long time afterwards, because it had a definite effect on him, precisely during the years in which he himself was preparing to be a minister of God. He understood, *sub contraria specie*, how sacramentals are to be imparted to God's people.

Thus we come to the celebration of the Holy Mass, which has no equal in the life of the Church. Right away we would like to say something fundamental that you know very well: the Mass is in the first place and above all the Sacrifice of Christ in sacramental form. It is not in the first place a sacred Banquet. It is also this, but is not primarily this. The purpose of these Spiritual Exercises would be fully achieved if we were to meditate for all the days to come on this truth alone. Today there is an urgent need for us priests above all to regain awareness of this truth taught by Sacred Scripture and constantly reaffirmed by the ecclesiastical Magisterium. We must celebrate the Mass remembering always that we are going up to Golgotha, to the altar and not to another place. An altar, in all cultures, is a sacred stone on which victims are sacrificed. When in the sacristy we are getting dressed for Mass, we should meditate on this:

> I am preparing to offer the immolation of the divine Victim. The blood of the Lamb of God will mystically sprinkle my priestly hands when I raise the Host. And I will hold that same sacrificial blood in the chalice, showing it to the faithful, and to myself, to adore him and thank him.

These are the spiritual sentiments that must precede, accompany, and follow the Eucharistic celebration. Let us form this habit, brothers: no talking in the sacristy! Nor is it the place to exchange pleasantries or make jokes. In the sacristy one prays. The sacristy is, in a certain way, a *pronaos*, meaning the part in front of the actual temple. It is a place of passage between the profane and the sacred. In the sacristy we must prepare ourselves for the encounter with God and with Christ, and we must prepare ourselves mystically to see our hands red with the blood of the Lamb, offered in expiation for sins. It seems that some of the mystic saints saw, at the exposition of the Host in the Mass, rivulets of blood come out of the Host itself and run down the hands and wrists of the priest. This is what happens mystically in the Mass! So how is it possible to turn it into a moment of laughter, of pranks, of unrelated matters? Only the lack of adequate doctrinal preparation, as well as the lack of a vision of faith regarding the Eucharistic Sacrifice, can give rise to these sorts of things.

The Mass is theocentric and Christocentric. This must also be visible somehow in the manner of celebrating. We have mentioned the orientation, including the physical orientation, of liturgical prayer. Today, in the vast majority of cases, the priest does not physically face the apse, a symbol of heaven, eternity, and Christ's return at the end of time. Today we are used to seeing the priest celebrate almost always, as it is called, "towards the people". We know that in itself celebration towards the apse or, as it is called, "towards the Lord", remains possible even with the Missal of Paul VI. Over many years, however, an ecclesial climate has been created on account of which if a priest celebrates the Mass of Paul VI in the national language but turned towards the apse during the Eucharistic Liturgy, he is immediately considered a sort of schismatic, extremist or ultratraditionalist. According to some, this liturgical posture is enough to make a priest someone who is not in "communion" with the Church. This is truly wrong and discriminatory.

We need to affirm that it is possible (and sometimes it is necessary) to celebrate very worthily even if the priest is facing "towards the people". But we must recognise that the possibility of celebrating "towards the people" does not represent one of the better elements of postconciliar liturgical reform. In a way, the Magisterium itself has indirectly pointed out its problematic character. Short of challenging the new practice, St John Paul II did however write that celebration "towards the people" requires greater spiritual maturity. What did he mean? He means that it is still possible to celebrate well even using this physical orientation. It is possible, but it is more difficult to stay in the presence of the Lord (1 S 6:20) and remain recollected in God. Furthermore, the symbolic character of the theocentric and Christocentric orientation of the Liturgy also disappears. In the Liturgy, in fact, we are not turned towards one another, but all towards the Lord. Benedict XVI recommended placing at least one crucifix in the centre of the altar, so that there is a sign that reminds both the priest and the faithful that even if we are physically turned towards each other, at least inwardly we must all be turned towards the Father and towards Christ, because Christ is the Christian east. Otherwise the Mass would not be worship, because it would not be adoration and prayer. Adoration and prayer can be addressed only to the Trinity, certainly not to ourselves or the community.

Now a priest who wishes to celebrate even the ordinary form of the Roman rite "towards the Lord" can do so, without having to ask anyone's permission. However, we are not unaware that today some of the world's bishops would make life impossible for such a priest. There are bishops who would require him under the bond of obedience to celebrate towards the people, and could even go so far as to relieve him of his duties if he should refuse to accept such an imposition. This gives food for thought: in an age in which certain bishops leave in place priests whose sins, even serious sins, are well known to them, a priest can however be removed from his post if he wants to do something that is good and (in any case) permitted by the Church: celebrating "towards the Lord".

In any event, what is always possible and necessary, even when celebrating "towards the people", is to do all one can to remain deeply recollected in God, entirely oriented towards the Lord. During this celebration, therefore, let us avoid all those attitudes and habits that may give the impression that the centre of our attention, while we are at the altar, is the assembly of the faithful. Of course, our little flock, the portion of the Church entrusted to us, is of fundamental importance for us priests. In giving our life to the Lord, we have in some way also given it to the faithful, to our people. We pray for them every day and are willing to sacrifice ourselves for those whom Christ wanted to entrust to us as children in the faith and in the Church. But when we are celebrating Mass, the best way to take care of our children is not to think about them but to draw them and lead them to die with Christ and live the new life with him!

Let us all recollect ourselves in God and in Christ. After all, the Liturgy itself prompts us to do this. Let us think of the prayers of the Mass. They are all addressed to God or to Christ. Not infrequently they begin by saying "Holy Father…" or "Almighty and eternal God…" or other such invocations. So, in saying those words, to whom are we talking? The prayers do not begin with "my dear children in Christ…" or "dear brothers…" No! At the altar we speak to God and to Christ, not to the faithful. And yet there are priests who, while reading those prayers, look at the gathered community, look at the people assembled there, as if they were speaking to them instead of to God! But this is an unwitting stumble into the ridiculous. Let's imagine that I find myself talking to a friend of mine named Antonio. We are sitting in the living room and I want to say to him, "Dear Antonio, I was thinking of going out for a walk." Imagine, however, that I said this as I turned towards the kitchen door, looking at my aunt who is there to prepare lunch. Antonio, of course, would say to me, "But where are you looking, who are you talking to? I'm right here!" Look, when we say prayers addressed to God but look at the people, we are doing something as absurd as in that example.

Let us also note that the Missal contains what are called the "apologetic prayers" or "secret prayers" of the priest. Although reduced in number, these are still found in the Missal of Paul VI, especially when the priest prepares for Holy Communion with the Body and Blood of the Lord. The rubrics require the priest to say these prayers in a very quiet voice, inaudible to the assembly. But if the words cannot be heard, why are they spoken? Because God hears them! The existence of these prayers is another proof of the fact that the Church wants the priest to pray during Mass, that is, to turn to God. This also seems trivial, but let us ask ourselves during these Spiritual Exercises: "When I celebrate Mass, do I pray? Am I talking with God? Do I look at him face to face? Do I let him look at me?" The Mass is the prayer par excellence. And yet we run the risk that for us it may be just a cold ritual, repeated thousands of times. No, dear brethren, we must pray during Mass, that is, we must meet with God and converse intimately with him.

Here, therefore, we discover this great theme: in the Liturgy, and above all in the Liturgy of the Mass, we find ourselves before the Tremendous Presence of the divine Majesty. The Liturgy celebrated well implies the perception of the Presence of God which makes us cry out like the prophet Isaiah: "Alas! I am lost, because I am a man of unclean lips, and I live among a people of unclean lips; yet my eyes have seen the king, the Lord of hosts" (Is 6:5). If we pray during Mass, if we contemplate and adore, then we realise what Holy Mass really is! And our way of celebrating, but also simply of moving in the sanctuary, even gestures such as sitting down, getting up, washing our hands... everything: everything will be transformed. Because we will be aware that there, at the altar, we are in front of the Presence that brings trembling and at the same time fills the heart with the love of God: the Presence of Golgotha, the Presence of Christ crucified and risen. If we perceive this in faith, we will not be able to remain indifferent. If we perceive it with a contemplative gaze, we will be able to embody the true *ars celebrandi*.

The art of celebration, in fact, does not consist only of the rigorous observance of rubrics and liturgical norms. This, obviously, is necessary. Indeed, it is so important that without observing the liturgical laws of the Church it would be impossible for us to attain the *ars celebrandi*. Observance of the norms, therefore, is not "rubricism", but obedience to the Church, and is a necessary and not an optional element of the *ars celebrandi*.

However, this observance alone is not enough. In fact, it is always possible to observe the norms scrupulously in order to carry out a formally perfect celebration in which, however, there is no personal encounter with Jesus; the face to face and intimate encounter with the Holy Trinity. So, for a true *ars celebrandi*, the observance of the norms must be joined by contemplation and the perception of the presence of God in Christ and in the Holy Spirit. Here once again is the theocentric and Christocentric character of divine worship. And this is not possible in huge concelebrations where the concelebrants chat with each other or take photographs and are very far, not only from the altar, but even more, far from God.

In this way, a good celebration of the Liturgy will truly be a source of sanctification for the priest, while on the contrary neglect of divine worship is never a sign of a stable and secure priestly path. In this we must invoke the help of three persons in particular: Mary, Joseph, and the woman of the Gospel who anointed Christ's feet with the precious ointment. Mary and Joseph took care of Christ's physical body on earth.

So too must the priest set his heart on safeguarding the Eucharistic Body of Christ, using all means necessary and the greatest possible care. The woman of the Gospel, now, used an entire jar of ointment of the highest value to anoint the feet of the Messiah. St John Paul II, in commenting on that episode, made the observation that, like that woman, the Church has never been afraid of "wasting" resources on liturgical worship. Indeed, the Church does not consider it a waste to invest resources for the dignity of the Liturgy.

Here again we can recall the figure of the Holy Curé of Ars, who went around in a patched-up cassock and shoes resoled several times, but bought very precious vestments for the celebration of Mass. We also remember that St Francis of Assisi, who went around barefoot and clad in sackcloth, wanted the churches of the Order he founded to have the most precious pyxes and chalices, because these were to contain the most precious Body and the most precious Blood of the Lord.

Naturally, here too it remains possible to follow these guidelines merely for the sake of aesthetic taste. In this case, the harsh words of the Lord would apply to us, when he says that the Jews wash the outside of the dish while the inside is full of iniquity. Caring only for the external apparatus of worship while our soul remains the den of the demons of sin who dwell there undisturbed would be not only useless, but even harmful. Instead, "new wine in new wineskins." Let us get the best for the external side of worship in such a way that, with God's help, the outward beauty of God's house may correspond to the interior clarity of our priestly soul. It is not only the sacred vestments and vessels that must shine, but the soul of the priest must also shine, reflecting the rays of the true sun, which is Christ. Thus God the Trinity will have two dwellings: the house of God which is the building, the church where worship is celebrated; and the house of God where he dwells, that is, the grace-filled soul of the priest who offers the immolation of Christ on the altar, every day, for the expiation of sins, for the salvation of the living and the dead.

Human, Spiritual, and Intellectual Formation in the Seminary and in Religious Life

As is evident, the years spent in a seminary or in a novitiate are years dedicated to formation in preparation for the priestly mission. *Pastores Dabo Vobis* of St John Paul II indicated four dimensions of this formation: human, intellectual, spiritual, and pastoral. The pastoral aspect has been excluded from the topic we are addressing, so we will mainly reflect on the other three aspects.

Several years ago, an Italian cardinal gave a lecture at a seminary, addressing precisely the question of the dimensions of formation. In his talk he asked the question, which was the principal dimension of the four. In fact, reasons could be given to support the primacy of each of the four over the remaining three. After some reflections, that cardinal concluded that in his view the most important dimension in priestly formation was the human dimension, because without it there would be no foundation for the other three. Since in a course of Spiritual Exercises we do not have to address, much less resolve, problems debated among specialists, it is not our intention to settle the question here. It is nonetheless possible to sympathise, at least to a limited extent, with the position expressed by that cardinal. It is, in fact, sure theological doctrine that grace does not eliminate nature, on the contrary it presupposes and elevates it. If grace presupposes nature, it somehow rests upon it. If nature is missing, what will grace be based on? If we apply this right and true principle to the sphere of formation, we could say that intellectual and spiritual formation (and also pastoral formation, which we will not speak of here) represent, so to speak, the side of grace. Intellectual formation, it is true, also includes human subjects, above all philosophy. But it is mainly theological formation, and theology is the science of faith, the science of supernatural realities, the knowledge of which is given to us by grace, through divine Revelation. Secondly, it is evident that spiritual formation equally points to the side of grace, as does pastoral formation, because pastoral care properly understood is never a simple human initiative, but is our co-operation with the Holy Spirit. Therefore these three dimensions point to the aspect of grace. The dimension of human formation instead points to nature, the formation of man as man.

Let us begin to meditate on this dimension. A priest (it seems silly to have to mention this) is before all else a human being. Every human being needs to be educated, but even before that, to be formed as a human being.

The family is primarily responsible for this human formation, then there is school and a few other social entities that also influence a person's education. We have already noted at the beginning that, unfortunately, more and more often the family of today in the West, at least in the majority of cases, no longer carries out its educational function as well as it did in the past. The family is often broken up or destroyed, but even when the parents are not separated, a mistaken way of understanding its own role often prevails, if not indeed a certain listlessness, almost a laziness on the part of parents who no longer want to go through the trouble and sacrifice of enduring the hard work it takes to raise a well brought up child, instructing him well, correcting him when necessary, and so on.

If we even so much as glance at schools, we see that in many cases things are no different. In the past a school, in addition to the necessary ideas, taught guidelines for life and behaviour; for example, it taught respect for the rules, timetables and authorities of the school. A boy or a girl did not grow up out of control, but received an education, was channelled as it were, put on track. They found out that one cannot do whatever one wants. They learned that there are roles in life that must be respected. For example, one learned that one must speak with respect to the teacher or the headmaster, that one cannot address them with the spontaneity with which one speaks to one's schoolmates. There are roles in society that must be respected. This was one of the great lessons of a classical education. Families and the school joined forces to bring children up well. People who are not quite so young, let's say forty years old and above, well remember that if they were reprimanded or punished at school, they prayed to God that their parents would not find out, otherwise once they got home they would get the rest! Today the opposite is often the case. Teachers are afraid even to say a word of reproof to pupils. If they do so, the next day the parents are likely to show up to protest, to threaten to file a complaint, or even, as has sometimes happened, to beat up the poor teacher! Children thus grow up with the idea of impunity: that is, that they can say and do whatever they want, and no one can punish them or even tell them off. Children today grow up with the idea that everything is a right and nothing is a duty. Many adolescents live in the belief that they are owed everything, while they do not owe anything to anyone. The fault lies with a mentality that has grown ever more deeply rooted in Western societies, a harmful pedagogical mentality, the appalling fruits of which are before our eyes every day, on the news.

The point is that we cannot think that seminarians, meaning future priests, come from the planet Mars. The seminarians and novices who arrive in formation today are also in the grip of this cultural context, and therefore a substantial number of them have not received the necessary human formation in their families and schools. The seminary will have to take care of this too, as far as possible, making up for lost time. It seems truly absurd, but today we have seminarians aged eighteen, twenty, or older who lack basic notions of personal hygiene, or how to sit at the table, or how to write a letter. Many do not even know where to write the address on an envelope or where to put the stamp. They have probably never sent a paper letter in their life, just e-mails. However, as priests, at least from time to time, they will still have to write and then post some traditional style letters, and they need to be prepared even for this kind of thing.

Many decades ago, there was a rather strict colonel in charge of a large barracks. Since e-mail did not exist at the time, all internal communication was made with forms filled out on a typewriter by a subordinate. Since in several cases the soldier who prepared those reports made mistakes in spelling or grammar, the colonel marked up the forms with the classic red and blue pencil and sent them back. He did this repeatedly, until he finally received a properly drafted report. Of course, we may think this man was very strict, but then again he was a soldier! Essentially, however, although he took it to extremes, he was right. Things must be done well.[2]

---

[2] There are not a few cases in which priests write to their bishop or send reports to the Curia and in reading them one realises the miserable state of the language in which they are written. Style, grammar, and spelling all leave much to be desired. Other priests send such letters by reusing old envelopes, crossing out the previous address with a pen and writing another...and this even if they are writing to their bishop. It will be said: why are we talking about these things in a course of Spiritual Exercises? Shouldn't we talk about the things of God and spirituality, instead of dwelling on envelopes, letters and postage stamps? In reality, it is true that we are not directly interested in these issues, but we cite them only as a sign of the fact that often the priest-man has not been formed in an adequate way of behaving, in a style worthy of a minister of God. This can be seen in many aspects: from the way of dressing, to that of walking, to the way of laughing and gesticulating, to the way of expressing oneself, and so on. Obviously, we are not advocating a "Galatean clergy": we do not mean, that is, that a well-formed priest needs to know by heart the famous work by Monsignor Giovanni Della Casa published in 1558. That book, *Il Galateo*, is in fact aimed at noble households rather than priests. What we mean to emphasise, rather, is that knowing how to behave well, including from a human point of view, is important for a priest.

There is in fact a right way and a wrong way of saying and doing things. This is part of human education. Very critical remarks are often made about the Roman Curia, and in some cases it may even be with good reason. There are, however, some positive things. One of these is the attempt to maintain a polite and deeply respectful style in relationships. For example, in curia meetings the established practice is to allow people to speak without interrupting them. Someone may disagree, but does not usually interrupt the person who is talking. At the end, when he has finished, comes the chance to respond, with a clear and polite explanation of the reasons for disagreement. So dialogue, even debate, is present. What is avoided as much as possible is rudeness. And all of this is good. How much more interesting and perhaps even useful would so many televised debates be if people simply observed good manners, waiting for their turn to speak. Instead we witness alleged debates that are no such thing. In fact, the word "de-bate" originally means "strike back". The idea is that one person strikes a blow and the other then strikes back. People take turns in speaking. First one speaks, then the other. But often on television this patience, this ability to listen, this education does not exist. Everyone yells, everyone constantly interrupts each other, everyone wants the upper hand. In the end, they all talk at the same time, nothing can be understood and nothing is accomplished.

Another sign of good manners is the use of the formal pronouns "lei" or, in certain areas, "voi". This too has disappeared in vast areas of the Western world and, as we have previously said, the informal "tu" is predominantly used. This habit is also taking hold in the Church, and it is not in all cases a good thing.

Let us conclude on this point. It is not our task to say whether human formation is or is not the most important of the four dimensions of priestly formation, but we can certainly say that it is urgent in our time and that many concrete problems arise because priests lack a solid formation at this level, and also on the pastoral level. For this reason, even when dealing with people in the parish or in other contexts, certain priests encounter difficulties or create problems for themselves precisely because they do not know how to behave correctly from a human point of view. Let us therefore question and examine ourselves today not only on the so-called "spiritual" things, but also on these human aspects. How do we behave in human terms? Do we know how to behave? Or should we grow and improve on this point? And in this case, what means must I use for my self-formation at the human level? What do I realise I need at this level? What people, what books could help me make up for lost time?

Very often, when reading the various websites and blogs that talk about Church matters, one encounters not only articles but also comments posted on them by Catholics, both priests and others. Many of these comments certainly make good points, they present sound doctrine...which is a good thing in any case. But many times, one notices omissions or outright insults in the way these Catholics express themselves, even about the Holy Father Francis or Benedict XVI. No one wants to deny current problems. But is it right to be violent, aggressive, and disrespectful in commenting on the situation? Is it really right to target an individual or a group, and lash out against them with a verbal violence that is almost unbelievable?

Let us rediscover, even as priests, the beauty of a well-mannered and orderly way of life, which in the past might have been called "chivalry". Unfortunately, when this word is used many people only think about good manners in relation to women, which is also important. But the term chivalry refers above all to the virtues of a medieval knight. According to experts on that historical period, the main virtues of a knight are: *prouesse, loyauté, largesse, courtoisie, franchise.* The first virtue is *prouesse*, meaning prowess. The knights had to possess superior martial skills, that is, to be skilled in battle, and strictly respect the rules. We remember that in the canticle of Moses and the Israelites we read, "The Lord is a warrior" (*Ex* 15:3). The knight's second virtue is *loyauté*, loyalty. The knight is loyal to God, king, country, and lady. The third virtue is *largesse*, meaning generosity. It indicates generosity of spirit, that is, the willingness to help those in material or spiritual need. Fourthly, there is *courtoisie*, courtesy. This virtue is embodied by maintaining impeccable language and behaviour. Finally, there is *franchise* or frankness. In reality, only by extension does this indicate speaking clearly, revealing one's mind when expressing oneself. Originally, the knight's frankness consisted in always maintaining an attitude in keeping with his rank and birth.

It is clear that these characteristics can be understood (and in fact have often been understood) in a purely worldly way, as court etiquette. But in their original inspiration, these values speak of something else. They outline the figure of a complete, dignified, honourable, respectful man. Not of a complicated man, but of a man of human substance, who has a solid human and moral structure, who has education, who has style (in the noblest sense of the term). We priests are certainly not called to live and behave like courtiers! However, we are called to be men who have style. A sober style, certainly, but at the same time a noble one, with that healthy nobility of spirit and behaviour which is unfortunately so often lacking in the way of life of many of our contemporaries. A dignified man does not speak and behave in certain ways, even if these are common in contemporary society. We often see painful cases in which priests, for example, appropriate ecclesiastical assets or assets belonging to the faithful. With cunning, they steal them from the Church or from the legitimate owners. Of course this is a sin, a violation of the seventh commandment. But even before that, it represents a human shortcoming, a lack of honour, of dignity. A priest who would do these or other despicable things, has he no love for his dignity, his honour, his rank? Does he not consider that his person, his name, his family, are tarnished when this or any other kind of wickedness is done? Or also in the way we dress, cut our hair, talk, move... do we have dignified behaviour in everything, are we well-mannered in all we do? It is not pointless to ask ourselves about these things. Perhaps we can use the aforementioned virtues of chivalry for an examination of conscience on our human dimension.

1. First of all, we must be brave. Are we courageous, or are we afraid of proclaiming the Church's doctrine and moral teaching with clarity, fidelity, and courage? When it comes to defending God, Christ, Our Lady, the Church, the needy, the downtrodden, do we do this with bravery, or do we just think of our quiet life and our precious privileges that we do not want to endanger?

2. Next, we must be loyal. What a beautiful gift loyalty is, in any man, but above all in a minister of God! And how many times it is betrayed! Loyalty is the virtue of friends. And it is the virtue that gives rise to thankfulness towards those who have done us good. But how often do priests break friendships even of many years' standing so as not to lose, perhaps, a career advancement? How many times are priests willing to betray, to hinder, to harm people with whom they have had a long friendship; and for what? How many times do we forget those who have done us good?

3. Then there is generosity. Even more than generosity in distributing material goods, this means generosity of heart. It is the attitude of the man who cultivates attentiveness to others, to their needs. It is the virtue of those who try to satisfy the legitimate requests they receive, who try to make people happy, to whatever

degree is possible. It is the gaze of someone who is not only benevolent towards those who ask, but even knows how to give more than is asked, perhaps before the request is made. This is what the Master says in the Gospel: "And if anyone forces you to accompany him for one mile, go with him two" (*Mt* 5:41). This is the generosity of heart of the Virgin Mary, who did not wait for Elizabeth to ask for help, but as soon as she learned that she was pregnant, spontaneously ran to give it. And Our Lady also does this for us from heaven. That is why Dante Alighieri puts these words in the mouth of St Bernard, referring to Mary: "Not only does your kindness help/those who ask, but many times/it voluntarily outruns the asking" (*Paradiso*, XXXIII, 16-18).

4. In the fourth place we cited courtesy. How beautiful it is when we meet gentlemanly priests! And, again, we are not referring to an outward gentility, which concerns only the bearing. We mean, instead, that gentility which warms the hearts of people who come into contact with it. A number of times we have had the experience of meeting these priests, particularly among those who today are older, who over the course of a long life have developed this sober and controlled but at the same time expansive human warmth that is able to warm hearts. How beautiful it would be if we too were to become capable of instilling this serene joy in those around us! This is done by behaving like gentlemen. Yes, the priest must have a noble bearing. Benevolence

and affection towards all, familiarity with none. Expressing ourselves correctly, with respect, even when our ministerial duty requires us to reprove someone for his conduct.

5. Finally, frankness, to be understood in the sense we gave above. We are nothing. But in spite of this the Lord has raised us to priestly dignity. No noble, no prince or king of this world possesses the dignity of being *alter Christus*, indeed of being *Ipse Christus*. Now, nobles show their birth and rank with suitable clothes, lavish dwellings, behaviour consistent with their status. We priests do not need castles and pages, but we too (in accordance with Christ's disciples) must be "frank", that is, we must manifest our birth in the sacrament of Holy Orders and the rank of ministers of Christ in which we have been placed. Poverty is a beautiful virtue. But let us not confuse it with shabbiness, lack of hygiene, or conforming to the fashions of the moment. There is a chivalrous frankness that must be observed in order that men, in talking with us, may always be aware of whom they have in front of them: a poor sinful man, but who is also a priest of Jesus Christ!

Let us therefore also meditate on the human dimension of our ministry and try to perfect it with God's help, in such a way that even its supernatural dimensions may rest on a more stable and solid foundation.

PART II

After dedicating this morning to meditation on human formation, let us now turn to the intellectual and spiritual formation of the priest.

The Church establishes that there be *curricula studiorum* preparatory to Sacred Ordination. With this practice, the Church recognises the importance of study for seminarians and novices, that is, it recognises the importance of the intellectual dimension in the ordained Catholic ministry. It is urgent to emphasise this in our age. We said this morning that we will not deal with pastoral formation. We must remember, however, that in large sections of the Church today there is an ultra-pastoralist tendency, which has, among its consequences, also that of denigrating the intellectual dimension of priestly life or giving the impression of ignoring or overshadowing the centuries-old doctrine and moral teaching of the Church. More or less clearly, it is thought (and sometimes said) that study not only does not help the priest to be a good minister of God, but on the contrary hinders his pastoral sensitivity. It is thought (and sometimes said) that a knowledgeable priest will not be a good shepherd of souls, because he will not be able to understand their frailty. He will be a priest with a systematised way of thinking who lives in the abstractions of his knowledge and will therefore not truly be able to get close to the people who, on the contrary, experience real problems every day.

Of course, there may be priests like that, but the generalisation that a cultured or at least educated priest cannot be a good shepherd or a good priest is certainly wrong. It should be enough to point out the Fathers and Doctors of Church history, who were excellent and holy ministers of God as well as great theologians and shepherds of souls, along with the other holy priests who, although not dedicated to professional study, took care to read and study a great deal, and this precisely in order to be priests more suited to their task.

There is also another element, which sometimes causes today's Church leaders to try to lower the bar on intellectual formation. That element is fear. Yes, fear! It is known that many parts of the world today experience the so-called "shortage of vocations". Many bishops are rightly concerned because they realise that each year the number of seminarians is much lower than the number of elderly priests who die. At this rate, they think, we will have to close almost all the parishes! One cannot help but share their concern. The bishops also know two other things. We have already mentioned the first: schools today are much less solid than they used to be. For this reason, many seminarians have not received an adequate basic cultural formation and have considerable difficulty when, in the seminary, they have to take courses and exams in philosophy and theology. A second thing the bishops also know (and it is above all a consequence of what we said about the state of families today) is that many seminarians get discouraged along the way and decide to leave the seminary, because to persevere amid the fatigue and difficulties seems to them an impossible undertaking.

As a result many bishops are worried and even afraid, saying, "The seminarians are few, and of those few, some of them leave." There are many reasons for leaving the seminary, but often it seems that the only one that can be remedied is academic discouragement. Essentially, many bishops try to arrange matters so that seminarians are not "frightened" by the professors and do not get discouraged on account of their studies.

There was one bishop who every now and then went to visit his seminary, where a theology programme was taught. During his visits, the bishop sometimes entered the classrooms where the courses were given, or strolled through the corridors and approached some of the professors, particularly the professors considered most demanding by the students. That bishop was amongst the ranks of the "frightened", and therefore said to the slightly more demanding professors: "Don't frighten the boys", "Don't let them get discouraged", "Turn a blind eye", "Don't be too demanding." In some cases, that bishop went so far as to say to some teachers, "You must pass all the students in the exams; you must never fail anyone!" In general, the professors were mostly priests from the same diocese or from neighbouring dioceses, so they either accepted these guidelines and conformed, or at least (if they did not want to follow these prescriptions) were silent when the bishop spoke to them this way. But one day one of them replied, "Your Excellency, you should thank me, because if I am demanding with the students, I am doing it for the Church and ultimately also for you, and certainly not for myself. If I am demanding and push them to study, in a few years you will have the best priests at your disposal, because they will be well prepared."

And indeed that teacher was right. As the saying goes, "Better a few, but good". Jesus knew that the harvest is plentiful, but the labourers are few, and yet he began with only twelve (*Mt* 10:36-37).

Anxiety over the numbers is understandable, but – as I wrote in my book *God or Nothing* – we should be concerned about the quality (certainly not only the intellectual quality, but including the intellectual quality) and the holiness of priests much more than we are about their numbers.

It is often said that, since the Holy Curé of Ars is the patron of priests with the care of souls (the majority of priests), such priests are dispensed from the duty of study, because it is known that the Curé d'Ars did not do well in theological studies and struggled to complete them. Now, it is true that the Curé of Ars did not have strong intellectual skills or at least did not do well in his studies, but this fact should not be exploited, for at least two reasons. A first reason is that if St John Marie Vianney was the great saint he was, this was due to his virtues and his commitment and certainly not to the lack of intellectual capacity or knowledge. He was holy because he co-operated with God's grace, not because he did not do well in school. Therefore, it is not a low intellectual level that makes a good priest.

In the second place, it should be added that the Holy Curé, although he did not possess high intellectual skills, indeed for that very reason, really applied himself to his studies! The hagiographers point out that there were more books in his rectory library than in the average library of a rural French parish priest of his time. In addition, bread crumbs have been found inside his books, a clue to the fact that he also dedicated his rare and frugal mealtimes to reading. In short, it would also be an historical error to say that priests are exempted from studying because the Curé of Ars did not study. That is not true! He was not particularly gifted as regards study, but how he studied! He studied to prepare his homilies and also catechism lessons for the people.

In these Spiritual Exercises, we have the opportunity to ask ourselves what our relationship with study is. A parish priest certainly cannot and should not spend three or four hours a day on books, unless he wants to do so and his duties leave him enough time. But for a priest involved in pastoral care not to study or at least read three or four hours a week is worrying! That would mean he doesn't even read for half an hour a day. And since from time to time the Magisterium offers us documents, priests will have to read them! It is true that it is not possible or necessary to read everything. A parish priest, if he does not have time, can limit himself to reading the encyclicals and little else, leaving minor documents aside. However, today many priests know the texts of the Magisterium only by hearsay or through a brief summary they have come across in some pastoral magazine.

Study is important. The priesthood, it is rightly said, is not a profession: it is a vocation. But in saying this, we mean that it is more, not less than an ordinary job. The priesthood is a God-given mission! So if a lawyer, a magistrate, a doctor, or an engineer must be very competent in order to do his job well, how much more must a priest be? If a doctor has not studied well, the sick die, if an engineer does not know his discipline, bridges fall down. And what happens to the souls entrusted to an ignorant priest? It is not surprising that St Teresa of Avila gave the following advice: even better than a holy spiritual director is an educated spiritual director, that is, one who knows what he is talking about. To direct souls, it is certainly necessary to have the right intention, but it is also necessary to know things. It is necessary to know the Word of God and the Magisterium, dogmatic theology along with moral and spiritual. We need to study!

Pope Francis proposed the effective metaphor of the Church as a field hospital. Few, however, reflect on what underlies this image. In the field hospital there is a need for highly skilled doctors who are able to save lives. A competent doctor is not formed in a day. Currently, at least in Italy, the medical school programme consists of six years of very demanding studies, in addition to another six years of specialisation. It takes twelve years of very serious and laborious studies to become a medical specialist. So good will is not enough to operate in a field hospital: it takes competence. And this is achieved by studying.

It is true that today there is also a theology or rather various theological movements that do not help the life and mission of the Church. We can imagine that it is this type of theologian the pope is thinking of, when he says he would like to put them all on an island, so that we can move forward. It is true: there are theologians of this type, theologians who deserve to be put on a desert island to discuss their abstract technicalities and their ideological questions. But it is not theologians as a whole, nor theology itself that is doing damage to the Church. On the contrary, what is harming the Church much more today is the widespread blind pragmatism of many clergymen. Pragmatism: thinking only about action. Blind, because it is not enlightened by consistent, solid thought, a thought based on the Word of God and the Magisterium of the Church. This pragmatism opens the way to all kinds of errors. It often cloaks itself in goodness, but in reality it is do-goodism. The shepherds who act this way, without constantly orienting themselves with the compass or beacon of the Word of God and the centuries-old moral teaching of the Church, are wolves in sheep's clothing. They say they serve the flock, but they want to use it for their own purposes.

During these Spiritual Exercises, therefore, let us make a serious resolution, almost a programme of daily study. As with all things, if we want to, we can do it. And as with all other things, so also with regard to studying: we must make the time to do it, otherwise the whirlwind of daily life will soon reabsorb our resolution and we will continue to act as before. It takes willpower, it takes sacrifice. Of course, this is not just a question of self-discipline, but of a response that we genuinely want to give to God's grace, which certainly invites us to be priests more capable of good service to the people of God. And to serve them well, we understand that we need more training, more reading, more study. Let us ask God in prayer for the willpower to carve out our little corner of study every day.

There are many priests in the world who do this and are very happy with it. They feel that the little corner they reserve for study, early in the morning or in the evening after closing the church, does a lot of good, allowing them to detach themselves from mere activity and retire in reflection, meditation, silent prayer. Furthermore, discovering new truths, learning more, makes us freer, always gives us a certain joy. There was a parish priest in Tuscany, a very active priest, very deserving, who was always among the people and had really made his parish into a family of families. In short, an edifying priest. He had made a tiny room in the sacristy where he had placed a number of books and a little desk. Around ten or eleven at night, when activities were over, he would retire there for an hour or more, until midnight, to read and study. He called it his "little garden". See, a priest with the care of souls, active, truly a good priest, who had carved out his intellectual garden and cultivated it every night. Can we do something like that too?

In Italy there is a fine saying: "Study ennobles". This is true. The study of good books ennobles the soul. And we know – also from our consideration of human formation – how important nobility of soul is for a priest. But in our case there is an even more important reason for study, because in general we priests study texts of theology and spirituality. These texts, then, put us in closer contact with God and with all the other truths of revelation and salvation history. As a private theologian, Joseph Ratzinger had taken up and developed something that is already found in St Bonaventure, where the Seraphic Doctor taught that the intellectual *habitus* of the theologian is born of the love that, as a Christian, he has for Christ. This position of Bonaventure and of Ratzinger after him is interesting. We know very well that St Thomas teaches that love is born of knowledge, rather than knowledge from love. In fact, we cannot love something or someone we do not know. And this is certainly true. But on the other hand, the process does not end here. If it is true that before loving we must know, it is also true that we then want to return from love to knowledge, because one of the effects of love is to make us want to know the one we love even better.

So love for God comes from knowledge of him. But then this love of ours in turn increases our knowledge, because we want to know the God we love better and more. Theology, then, is certainly science, that is, systematic knowledge; we could even say professional knowledge of the Word of God. But theology is a science in love with its object, which is God revealed in Christ. Theology arises not only from a speculative end, but rather from both a speculative end and a volitional one. In fact, the movements we mentioned above, those recent movements that, instead of helping, pull us away from faith, they are characterised precisely by being very technical, specialised reflections, where however love for the loved object is lacking and, as a result, so is love for the recipients of one's theology, for the readers who are none other than the Catholic faithful whom the theologian should be helping better to contemplate the face of God.

These reflections represent an encouragement for us, but again also an opportunity for an examination of conscience. If we are completely indifferent to reading and studying books concerning the things of God, is this not a worrying sign of uninterest, of coldness not only towards the books but also towards the One about whom these books are written? If we love God and Christ, we want to know more about him and about all the things he has done and is doing in salvation history. This is why the founder of one religious institute tried to urge its younger members on, saying, "There is so much more to know! You should thirst to learn more!"

These observations are already leading us to the spiritual dimension of priestly formation, since, for us priests, study is never just a purely intellectual experience, but also remains always an activity that we carry out in the love of Christ and in order better to serve Our Lord. Time has passed quickly in making these nonetheless brief observations on the intellectual dimension, which is why, when we come back, we will take up the topic of the spiritual dimension, which is perfectly suited for a meditation on the spiritual dimension of our formation.

To conclude, let us invoke the Holy Spirit through the intercession of Mary, Mother of Wisdom. Let us pray that he will always grant us his gift of knowledge and his gift of wisdom. A mind enlightened by a better understanding of God's truth will be better able to offer souls a light on the path to holiness.

Veni, Sancte Spiritus. Veni, per Mariam.

Priestly Life and Ascetic Life

PART I

The previous reflection brought us to the theme of the spiritual formation of priests. It is well known that, among theologians, there has been and still is a certain debate on the precise definition of spirituality. What does "spiritual life" mean for us Christians? We are well aware that we are not called here to settle disputed issues, moving instead on the level of meditation and contemplation. We can therefore start from a vision of spiritual life that focusses on the essential. Normally, the essence of a reality is indicated by its definition, but also simply by its name. So it is in our case as well, in the case of Christians. Perhaps we take it for granted that the many goods we have received in Baptism include this: the possibility and the honour of applying to ourselves the name of Jesus Christ. In fact, since the time of the New Testament we have simply called ourselves "Christians". This may seem trivial, but it is not. We all know very well, and believe, that our God, the only true God, is the Most Holy Trinity.

Yet Providence did not establish that we should call ourselves "Trinitarians", but rather "Christians". This is our name, which also indicates the essence of our religious life (*Ac* 11:26; 26:28; *1 P* 4:16). Our course of Spiritual Exercises has been given this title as its theme: *Jesus said to him: "I am the way, the truth and the life; no one comes to the Father except through me"* (*Jn* 14:6). These words of the Lord say it all. In them is the essence of Christianity, if it is legitimate to express oneself in these terms.

In these words is the presence of Christ Jesus, the Son, and of the Father. Hence there is reference to the intra-Trinitarian link between the First and Second Person. Other texts of the New Testament then teach us how essential the role of the Holy Spirit is for our contact with Christ: we considered this aspect before. Therefore, with a view that extends to the whole of the New Testament, we can say that in these words of Jesus there is reference to God, to the Trinity.

We also have to mention another detail. According to various exegetes, when Jesus says, speaking in an absolute way, "the Father", the Lord is not really referring to the First Person only, but to God (and therefore to the Three Persons). In fact, according to this exegesis, when Christ wants to refer to the Father in the strict sense, meaning the First Person of the Trinity, the Master does not absolutely say "the Father", but rather "my Father", thus indicating that I-You relationship which realises and manifests the distinction in the divine nature. If this exegesis is correct, it reinforces, on the basis of the same text of

John 14:6, what we are saying: that in these words Jesus is referring to God as Trinity.

Then, in the same words, there is the clear Christological reference: no one comes to the Father – or we can say no one comes to God – except through me (*Jn* 14:6). Christ is absolutely the only way to get to know God. It is always surprising to read the work of some recent theologian who tries to show that there are alternative ways of revelation or salvation, parallel or in competition with respect to the only Way, which is Christ Jesus. One wonders what "spirit" could inspire such theological ventures. It is difficult to think that this is the Holy Spirit or even just an upright spirit of faith. But again, rather than theological questions themselves, we are concerned here with their spiritual implications. On a spiritual level, in fact, it makes a big difference whether we firmly believe that Jesus is the only Way of knowledge and access to the mystery of God or accept the error according to which there are other ways.

With these references we have already got to the bottom of what spiritual life is for us. For us, who call ourselves Christians, spiritual life is Christ. Jesus says so in this very verse, where, in addition to the Truth and the Way, he defines himself as the Life. St Paul says: "For me, to live is Christ" (*Ph* 1:21). "I have been crucified with Christ, and it is no longer I who live, but Christ lives in me. And this life I now live in the flesh I live by faith in the Son of God, who loved me and gave himself for me" (*Ga* 2:20). On a strictly literal level, if we consider just the context of the passage, the apostle is referring to physical life on earth. But we know that the Bible should not be read only on a literal level, so this verse has always been interpreted in reference to spiritual life as well. Spiritual life for us is Christ. Leading a Christian spiritual life means, in its essence, being bound to Christ or, even more than bound, "grafted" into Christ like the branches of the vine (*Rm* 11:16-24; *Jn* 15:1-8).

Spiritual life therefore means first of all living in the grace of God, remaining grafted on the vine in order continually to receive the vital spiritual sap. We do not save ourselves on our own. We need the stream of divine sap, that is, of grace, to flow within us, coming to us as a gift from the vine, Jesus. So in these Spiritual Exercises we must make the firm resolution, with the help of divine grace, to will to persevere always in remaining in intimate union with Christ. More concretely, during these Exercises we want to confirm our determination to hate mortal sin with all our strength. Let us pray that the Lord may grant us holy disgust for sin. Let us ask the Holy Spirit that, in the face of the possibility of sinning, we may feel a true inner revulsion. Let us recall again those marvellous words of Chrysostom, according to which the priest must shine as if he were a sun, reflecting the light of Christ. Let us not allow the mirror of our soul to be dulled by venial sin. But more than anything, let us do all we can to keep mortal sin from shattering the mirror of the soul, such that it would become almost incapable, except in a very fragmented and ineffective way, of reflecting the face of Christ.

Spiritual life is keeping the mirror of the soul intact and clean, so that Christ may be mirrored in it and the luminous rays emanating from the face of Christ, rebounding from our soul, may generously reach other men and attract them to heavenly truth and beauty.

Future priests must be formed for all of this. Spiritual formation must start from this basis: there is no true Christian spiritual life where Christ is offended, we could say cast out by mortal sin. God and sin are incompatible. It is pure illusion or falsehood to teach that even in the presence of mortal sin, especially if this sin is not an accident but a stable condition, there could still be a fruitful Christian spiritual life. How can the branch bear fruit, give the delicious clusters of grapes, if it is cut off from the vine? Jesus says, "Without me you can do nothing" (*Jn* 15:5). Truly, without him we can do many things: many bad things or at least things having nothing to do with eternal salvation. But something good, holy, and valid for eternal salvation, this we can do only if we are inhabited by the Holy Trinity through Jesus Christ. Otherwise we would be presuming to save ourselves with our merely human good works.

Initial spiritual formation, which indeed has to be prolonged throughout the whole span of our priestly life, must therefore aim above all at this: to make us discover union with Christ and to make us persevere in it, with the help of grace. The seminarian and then the priest is not just a man who lives for Christ, that is, to serve him. Of course he is also this, but there is more. The priest lives for Christ, with Christ, and *in* Christ, and Christ lives *in* him. There is a mutual belonging. In the preceding days we have said that priestly spirituality does not cancel but instead confirms the full masculine character of the priest. This is why we said that it seems more suited to the masculine psychology of the priest to live a spousal union with the Church. But this spousal union with the beautiful Woman-Church is still an offshoot of the soul's fundamental union with Christ. In fact, being grafted into Christ is lived concretely in being incorporated into his Mystical Body. The "marriage" – so to speak – of the priest with the Church is a consequence of the indwelling of the Trinity in his soul through the Supreme and Eternal Priest, that is, the only Mediator, Jesus Christ. Thus our spiritual life takes shape, at the same time, as life in Christ and in the Church, as well as life for Christ and for the Church. If there were only the latter without the former, the risk of functionalism would be evident. This risk is however absent when, although we work and exert ourselves for the Lord and for his Mystical Body, we do so as an inevitable consequence of our being in them. Doing must always have a secondary place with respect to being.

Starting from the seminary years, it is important to inculcate this vision in future priests, so that they can hold onto it throughout their lives. It is the vision according to which it is necessary first to be with the Master, to spend time with him, "to remain with him" (*Jn* 1:39). Only afterwards can we be sent on mission, always by him. We all remember well how the Gospel puts it: "He appointed twelve – whom he called apostles – to be with him and to be sent out to preach" (*Mk* 3:14).

So here is a point for prolonged meditation, both during the time we have left in these Spiritual Exercises and in the following days and months, asking ourselves the essential question: "How much time do I spend with Jesus?" We are referring to the time during the day that each of us dedicates exclusively to Jesus. Let us go over the schedule of a typical day in our minds: how much time is reserved solely for Jesus Christ? Perhaps, examining our schedule carefully, we will be amazed at how little time it is, especially when compared with the time dedicated to other activities or to leisure. Naturally, with the mentality prevalent today in some sectors of the Church, to this question of ours some would immediately object: "It is not quantity that counts, but quality." Far be it from us to say that quality is not important. It certainly is. But are we sure that quantity and quality are contradictory elements, so either there is one or there is the other? Are we certain that, in order to elevate the quality of our moments of encounter with the Lord, we must reduce their number and duration?

Today this thought crosses the minds of many, even some priests. It is thought that if things are repeated too often or take too long, they end up being boring. Therefore, according to this vision, it would be better to reduce the number and duration of times for prayer so that, when we pray, that moment is more enjoyable. The basic idea is that the lower the frequency and duration (that is, the lower the quantity) of prayer, the greater the quality, meaning the intensity, spiritual savour, and fruit. This implicitly presents quantity and quality as contradictory. The Catholic philosopher Romano Amerio, addressing this mentality, wrote instead that quality and quantity are distinct but not contradictory. They are distinct because there can be quantity without or with little quality and, conversely, high quality in little quantity. However, Amerio recalled, very often quantity and quality go together. And he gave the example of study, saying, "To study well, I have to study a lot." That is, if I want to reach a high level of knowledge and specialisation, I have to devote many hours a day, and for many years, to studying. The quantity of study will produce quality. And if this does not happen in all cases (because there may be someone who studies a lot but does not have much acumen), it remains true that producing quality in study takes a great quantity of time devoted to intellectual work.

Let us apply this to prayer, to our moments of encounter with Christ. Of course we are interested above all in the quality of our spiritual life and do not set ourselves with stopwatch in hand to mark how much time we have dedicated to prayer, thinking that quantity alone can save us. But paying attention to quantity, as we have noted, is also important in view of the quality of the spiritual life. How many hours a day are dedicated to meeting the Master? While praying in the garden of Gethsemane, Jesus says to the sleeping apostles, "So you were not able to watch with me for one hour? Watch and pray, so as not to fall into temptation. The spirit is willing, but the flesh is weak" (*Mt* 26:40-41). The Spiritual Exercises are a truly propitious time not only to pray more during the days they occupy but also to make decisions, firm resolutions to increase the amount of time each day that we dedicate exclusively to meeting Christ in prayer and adoration. The Exercises must be a spark that sets off a fire destined to burn afterward. Otherwise the Spiritual Exercises would be a flash in the pan.

The seminary or novitiate are of great help because they impose schedules of daily prayer. But even there, the seminarian or novice is called to add something of his own; he is called to multiply the opportunities for prayer. He must learn to pay frequent visits to Jesus present in the tabernacle in order to build a true, personal and intimate friendship with Jesus. For example, in many seminaries there is a community celebration of the Liturgy of the Hours, at least the main hours. In various seminaries, Lauds and Vespers are recited together. In others, Midday Prayer and Compline are also added. However, it seems that there are few seminaries where the Office of Readings is also recited every day. It is highly recommended that seminarians add this recitation on their own, in part so that they may form the habit of fidelity to reciting the Office, which they will take on as a daily duty with diaconal ordination. Another example concerns personal devotions. In many seminaries the Holy Rosary is recited as a community once a week, while in others only during the months of October and May. But it seems there are few seminaries where this is scheduled every day. Here too, therefore, the seminarian must reserve time during the day, every day, for the Rosary. It is such an important devotion that we really cannot imagine a priest who does not recite every day at least five mysteries of the Holy Crown of Mary, a very powerful spiritual weapon as well as a "tower of salvation amid the assaults of hell", as Blessed Bartolo Longo calls it in the *Supplication to Our Lady of Pompeii*.

The purpose of the spiritual formation given in the seminary or novitiate is to ensure that the future priest be a man of God, a man of prayer, and a man who stands always before the Lord. How important this is! That we be, and also be recognised by others as, men of God. We can think of the example of many holy priests who have consumed their lives like the lamp before the tabernacle. Let us think of the many parish priests, from all places and all eras, who have spent their lives adoring Jesus in the tabernacle and serving their faithful, day after day, in the task assigned them. It is always so edifying when, entering a church, we find the parish priest praying in front of the tabernacle. Unfortunately, this is a scene rarely witnessed today. But there are still priests who have understood and put into practice the aforementioned verse of the Gospel: "He appointed twelve – whom he called apostles – to be with him and to be sent out to preach" (*Mk* 3:14). These priests have understood that they have been chosen and appointed not simply to go and preach, but to be with Christ and then also to preach. These holy ministers of God have understood that they need to spend time alone with Christ. To give the Master time, so the Master may speak to their heart. Thus they realise every day what God says about Israel in a famous prophetic passage: "I will lead her into the desert and speak to her heart" (*Ho* 2:16). Spiritual life is letting God lead our soul into the desert, meaning a silent and isolated place, a place where there are no others, a place for meeting none but God. That place, in which God speaks, is our soul, our heart. Every day, in front of the tabernacle, we find this desert of silence, of holy solitude, where God speaks to each of us face to face as a man speaks to his friend (*Ex* 33:11). God's word makes this desert a garden of delights, the Eden of an encounter with him.

Spiritual life is the prerequisite for pastoral life. To be with Christ, hearing him, listening to him, seeing him, contemplating him, touching him is the *conditio sine qua non* for being able to speak of Christ and do the works he has entrusted to us:

> That which was from the beginning, which we have heard, which we have seen with our eyes, which we have looked upon and touched with our hands, concerning the word of life – the life was made manifest, and we saw it, and testify to it, and proclaim to you the eternal life which was with the Father and was made manifest to us. (*1 Jn* 1:1-2)

Yes, we may be very good at talking about Jesus Christ because we have studied or have read books. We act as teacher but not as witness, as competent scholar and scientist but not as the man who has met Jesus in prayer and in silent contemplation. Let us recall the reading of the Office for the liturgical memorial of St Dominic, where it is said that if he was not speaking with God he was speaking of God. In that reading, taken from the *History of the Order of Preachers*, we read that the founder of the Dominicans "was very frugal of words and, if he opened his mouth, it was either to speak with God in prayer or to speak of God". This was the norm that he followed and also what he recommended to his brothers. We cannot speak of Jesus Christ if we have not first contemplated him, seen him with our eyes and touched him with our hands (*1 Jn* 1:1).

Prayer is necessary for preaching. Otherwise we would be like clanging cymbals. Many ministers of the Church speak of God without first speaking with God. Jesus says that the mouth speaks from the fullness of the heart – *ex abundantia cordis os loquitur* (*Mt* 12:34). This abundance of the heart that our Master speaks of is certainly not a human rhetorical skill! The heart is not to be filled with "communication strategies" designed by committee. The heart must be filled with the Presence of God. From this abundance the heart speaks! And without spiritual life, without spending time with Christ, the heart remains cold and empty. And so do our words. Words will not be lacking (we priests are never at a loss!) but they will be empty words, superficial, pleasant to men but not persuasive gifts. How many priests without any spiritual life can speak very well! But what is their fruit?

It is said that one day some neighbouring parish priests said to the Curé of Ars, "We preach the Forty

Hours, the homilies for the Ember days, the parish Spiritual Exercises, and many other initiatives. We invite famous preachers to speak to the people and, at times, we even bring great professors from the Sorbonne...yet our initiatives are not as successful as yours. You give simple homilies, you do not have much education, but the fruits are enormous..." It appears that the Holy Curé cut short this line of reasoning with a simple question: "But do you work on your knees?" This is the point. The homilies of the Holy Curé of Ars were certainly less polished and less theologically structured than those of the great preachers of his time. But his words came from a heart overflowing with the Presence of God, from the heart of a priest who spent many hours a day kneeling before Jesus in the Host.

Let us take this question of St John Mary Vianney seriously, as one addressed to ourselves. Let us imagine the Holy Curé personally asking each of us: "It seems to you that the fruits of your ministry are scarce or at least fewer than expected. You do not feel satisfied... but you, dear brother, do you work on your knees?"

Let us pray to Our Lady to inspire us with true devotion to her Son, so that we may learn to appreciate the importance of being with him in order to serve him well.

PART II

What we have said represents an indispensable prerequisite for meditating on the theme "Priesthood and ascetic life". As we know, spiritual theology is usually divided into ascetical theology and mystical theology. Simplifying, we could say that mystical theology studies the gifts of grace that God gives to the soul on the spiritual journey, from the most widespread and common gifts to the rare gifts reserved by God for some chosen souls that we usually call mystics. Ascetical theology, for its part, reflects on what the soul does to co-operate with grace within a complete Christian spiritual life, in which God's grace and man's freedom meet.

With this distinction in mind, we could say that without mysticism there can be no true ascetics. To understand this concept better, let us reflect on another area of faith, namely divine revelation. We know very well that the fundamental difference between Christianity and other religions consists in the fact that other religions are attempts that men have made, so to speak, "from below", to discover God or the gods and to worship them. Christianity, on the other hand, is the true religion because it was not created by men, but was revealed "from above", by God himself. John's Prologue teaches: "No one has ever seen God; the only begotten Son, who is God and in the bosom of the Father, he has revealed him" (*Jn* 1:18). And in the Gospel of Luke the Lord confirms: "Everything has been given to me by my Father and no one knows who the Son is but the Father, nor who the Father is but the Son and he to whom the Son wishes to reveal him" (*Lk* 10:22). This is why the religions of the world, although they contain some elements of truth, are not the true religion of the true God. God remains, in fact, inaccessible to men, unless he wants to reveal himself to them (*Ex* 33:20-23; *1 Tm* 6:16; *1 Jn* 4:12); Christ reveals God (*Jn* 6:46; 14:6-11; *Mt* 11:27); God is truly known, in depth and in full truth, only if he grants such knowledge. Otherwise, to human capacity the divine mystery remains inaccessible.

Let us now return to the relationship between gifts of grace and our co-operation in the spiritual life. The criterion remains the same: we cannot have a true spiritual life simply "from below", that is, by imposing on ourselves a self-discipline that we call asceticism. If that were the case, Christianity would not be much different from certain Asian religions in which men inflict hard trials and privations on themselves in order to achieve the most perfect concentration. In these religious models, man's concentration is essential precisely because he thinks he can find the divine (whatever concept he may have of it) by descending into the depths of his own interiority. It is true that St Augustine seems to say things like this, for example in his famous expression *noli foras ire, in teipsum redi: in interiore homine habitat veritas* (do not go outside, go back within yourself: the truth dwells in the inner man). This phrase, however, must not be misunderstood. To understand it correctly, it must be situated within the whole of Augustinian thought. And it is not by chance that we find it in the work *De vera religione* (39.72). It is very clear that for St Augustine, only Christianity is the true religion and that we have received the true religion from God. For Augustine it is evident that Christianity is not the fruit of our human reflections. In fact, for many years he had followed a philosophical path, but he found peace for his restless heart only in our religion given "from above". When the African Doctor says that we should not look outside but rather within ourselves, he is only saying that God makes himself known in our souls, even more than he does by means of external creatures. This is a spiritual method that is clearly influenced by a Platonic view. In no way, however, is Augustine suggesting that we find Christianity with techniques of concentration. He says only that God is in the depths of the heart, where we taste the savour of truth.

All this allows us to reach our goal: to recall that in the spiritual life asceticism is not a form of self-salvation "from below". There can be asceticism in the Christian sense only as a second phase, as a response to the grace of God that anticipates, arouses, accompanies and leads to completion the effort made by human freedom. Framing things properly in this way, then yes: we can and must value asceticism in our priestly life.

We would like to simplify many things that could be said about priestly asceticism into these short words: for us priests, cultivating ascesis means learning that we cannot do and say whatever we want. For us, ascesis is becoming aware that, by accepting the priestly vocation, we have decided to belong totally to Christ and to be used by him as he pleases. We have also chosen something else, namely representing Christ in the midst of men. St Paul says: "I have been crucified with Christ, and it is no longer I who live, but Christ lives in me" (*Ga* 2:20). St James tells us, "Speak and act as persons who are to be judged according to a law of freedom" (*J* 2:12). But what is the freedom of the Christian, and above all, the freedom of the priest? St Paul explains this very well also: "You in fact, brothers, have been called to freedom. Do not, however, allow this freedom to become a pretext for the flesh; but through love be at the service of one another" (*Ga* 5:13). And elsewhere the same apostle of the Gentiles writes, "[You say,] 'All things are lawful for me!' Yes, but not all things are helpful" (*1 Co* 6:12).

The asceticism that is imposed on us therefore consists in learning true priestly freedom, the freedom of the children of God construed in the particular role of the priest. St James reminds us that we must be able to speak and act according to this law of true freedom, of that freedom which does not at all consist in saying or doing whatever we want, but rather in saying and doing whatever allows Christ, whose unworthy representatives we are, to shine through our speech and our actions. In the Letter to the Ephesians, St Paul writes, "I tell you therefore and I adjure you in the Lord: do not behave any more like the pagans with their vain thoughts" (*Ep* 4:17). And a little further on he adds, "Let no evil words come out of your mouth, but rather good words that can serve for opportune edification, benefiting those who listen" (*Ep* 4:29). As we see, the apostle is referring precisely to a way of acting and a way of speaking that cannot be out of control. The synthesis of all this is again in the same chapter 4 of Ephesians, where he writes:

> But you did not so learn to know Christ, if indeed you have listened to him and been instructed in him, according to the truth that is in Jesus, to abandon with its former conduct the old man who is corrupted by following the deceitful passions, and to be renewed in the spirit of your minds, and to put on the new man, created according to God in true righteousness and holiness. (*Ep* 4:20-24)

Of course, these words apply to all the baptised, but they make a special appeal to priests, because from those who have been given more, more also is asked. Now, in what will our priestly asceticism consist? In no longer acting as we did before. And we are not referring only to mortal sin, which obviously has no place in our life. We are also referring to things that are in themselves lawful or neutral if done by others, but are out of tune with the life of a priest.

Let us look at some examples. There are priests who as young men, before entering the seminary, played a musical instrument and went around giving concerts. After being ordained they continue on their music tours. And this is not a matter of participating in festivals of religious songs. There are other priests who before entering the seminary dressed in tight and perhaps ripped jeans. And they want to continue to dress like that even as priests. There are priests who used to wear bracelets, bangles, rings, and in some cases, even earrings. Unfortunately, there are some cases of priests with earrings, but thank God they are rare. Priests are however often seen wearing jewellery of various kinds. The examples could go on.

What do we mean by this? That some habits lawful or neutral in themselves nevertheless do not suit the priest. Playing an instrument in a band and giving concerts is not a sin. But it does not suit a priest. We must leave behind many of our past habits in order to make room for our Christological representation above all else. When men see us, they must – however indistinctly – be able to see Christ. There are even some foul-mouthed priests who often and willingly resort to lewd language, not to mention vulgarity. Some priests tell dirty stories and pepper their speech with innuendos of a sexual nature. Perhaps they think that in this way they will get "closer" to young people. They may get closer, but they will not lead them anywhere other than their current state. The priest must instead coax them out, he must help the fledgling to fly. But if he speaks and acts like everyone else, where is the difference? It is true that many people rejoice and take pleasure in meeting priests with a quirky and breezy style. When a priest arrives who behaves like this, he often garners approval and affection. If a priest then uses bad language, the young people fawn over him. But this is at the superficial level. When the time comes in which the faithful really need a priest for serious matters, for deep spiritual needs, they will by no means turn to that priest. The same people who just moments before thought him likeable and bubbly will say to themselves, "I'm definitely not going to that clown!"

Another offshoot of our priestly asceticism, which implies self-discipline and even constant self-censorship, must be exercised in our public statements, both in homilies and catecheses and also through the social media platforms and blogs that number many priests as their users. Each of us naturally has personal opinions, for example in the political sphere. There is a strong temptation to use the church pulpit or any pulpit given to us as priests (whether material or digital) to spread our own ideas rather than the doctrine of the Church. This is frequently seen and is a serious matter. If we are given a pulpit, if people pay attention to us, it is because we are priests. In a certain sense, our being there comes from no merit of our own. People listen to us because they want to listen to Christ and the Church. This is why Jesus said, "Whoever listens to you listens to me" (*Lk* 10:16). It is truly sad, then, that a homily or catechesis should become a political rally or occasion for pseudo-theological indoctrination. Priestly ascesis implies that we watch what we say to the faithful.

With respect to this too, we must live as new men, that is, put on the new man created according to God in righteousness and true holiness (*Ep* 4:24). As private citizens, we vote and everyone can have his own candidate or party of preference. But let us not split our Christian communities! If I am on the left on a personal level, I must remember that some of my faithful are on the right. Conversely, if I am on the right, I must not alienate the faithful on the left. I can be in complete disagreement on a political level with what some faithful in my community think, but my relationship with them is that of a father to his children, not of a majority party to the opposition. How many pointless rifts are created in the body of believers for political reasons! And how sad it is when the homily presents content found not in the Catechism but in the newspaper that takes the priest's preferred editorial line. The faithful on the other side will feel alienated, excluded, sometimes even judged. All because that priest does not want to watch over his conduct and his words.

Another application of the same principle concerns ecclesial groups. A number of priests are members of an ecclesial group or movement, or they sympathise with it. Nothing wrong with that. But here too it must be remembered that a priest is ordained for all the faithful, not just for those of his ecclesial group. In some cases, this even reaches the point of contempt towards those who frequent a different ecclesial movement, in particular if it has a different perspective. This too is a political way of seeing the Church. It is clear that orthodoxy and orthopraxy must be protected, so if these are in danger in a certain movement or association the Church must intervene. But when this is not the case, there has to be more charity. Even "that other lot" are my baptised brothers! I have the right not to agree with their theological or ecclesial vision, but as long as they do not deny defined doctrine or promote immorality, I must love and value what they do, because this is another dimension of the wealth of Church, which I may be lacking. This does not mean having no thoughts. Instead it means having, in addition to thoughts, a heart as well.

Today in the Church one often witnesses terrible internal strife. We recall that Benedict XVI, well aware of the situation, in a meeting with the Roman clergy quoted the passage from St Paul that says, "If you bite and devour each other, at least take care that you do not completely destroy each other!" (*Ga* 5:15.) Those who read ecclesial news blogs and articles know what we are talking about. Above all, in reading the comments that so many Catholics add to such news stories and articles, one notices how often there is a real anger, the fruit of ideology rather than faith, that characterises such comments. Let us always remember, brothers, that it is fitting and right to have opinions, to have positions. It is certainly possible to express criticism. In some cases, indeed, this is necessary. We have the right to feel sorrow when we see wrongdoing in the Church. Sorrow, yes; but not anger. When one reacts with anger, this means that something is amiss. And let us also remember that the things of God are not to be spoken of with hatred. Let us denounce the error if necessary. But let us not lose charity. "Rather, speaking the truth in love, we are to grow up in every way into him who is the head, into Christ" (*Ep* 4:15).

Ascesis is an essential exercise, especially today when little value is attributed to this aspect of Christian life. We say especially today, because the younger generations of priests have not been educated in asceticism as in the past; and paradoxically it is precisely these generations

140

that need it most. Why? Why on earth would young priests need it more? For two main reasons: the first is that the world today offers infinitely more occasions for mortal sin than in the past. And the second concerns a point already dealt with over the past few days: many young priests are undoubtedly generous and mean well, but through no fault of their own did not receive as solid an education at home and school as was given in the past. This solid education included the aspects of speech, posture, dress and, above all, the sense of duty and the capacity to sacrifice. All truly important things in the life of a priest. So we need to relearn them, we need to acquire them if they were not given to us or develop them if they were offered to us in an insufficient way. Ascesis allows all of this.

In particular, ascesis does this because it is the practice of deprivation and sacrifice. I would like to sleep or go for a stroll, but no: duty calls me! This is a true ascetic act. I would like to post on social media whatever comes to mind, but no: I have to reflect and weigh my words carefully, because I have to edify and not scandalise. This is ascesis. I would like to avoid controlling myself in the way I speak when I am in public, I would like to say anything I want and I would like to inculcate my personal opinions in people's minds, but no: I have to talk about Christ, not about myself. A great ascetic act. I would like to avoid doing corporal penances regarding food, drink, luxuries, sleep; but I understand that these things really do make me grow.

In a society in which many people are willing to make enormous sacrifices to follow a diet for the sake of the perfect shape, for purely aesthetic reasons, many of us are unable to offer even the smallest renunciation in food or drink. There is an appalling spiritualism: it is thought and said that "the heart is enough" and there is no need to do corporal penance. This is not true! Both are needed, both interior and exterior penance. The exterior, without the interior, would be Pharisaic. But this means only that we must always keep the two together; it does not mean that external penance can be dispensed with. Here is another point for us to examine during the Spiritual Exercises. Do I give something up in food, drink, clothes? Every now and then, do I get up at night to pray for half an hour and keep Jesus company? Am I willing to make a few sacrifices for love of him? Am I willing to offer something to my Master?

Let us repeat: without some corporal penance, we run the risk of being spiritualistic, not spiritual. A bishop once had no choice but to go to a good restaurant for dinner during Lent. He paid close attention to what he ordered, because he had made penitential resolutions. He did not order wine, drinking only water. Moreover, he chose simpler dishes than the other diners did. At the end of the dinner, it was time for dessert and everyone ordered it. The bishop, however, asked for fruit. He tried to keep the others from noticing these little sacrifices, but this was impossible and everyone realised that he was observing little Lenten "florets", as they are called here in Italy. Faced with the evidence, the bishop had to admit that this was so, and he added: "You know, I remain convinced that in some way penance must not be only spiritual; it must be felt in the body. These are very small things, but it is necessary to feel a little inconvenience in the body, a little renunciation. A purely spiritual fast would not be enough for me; I think that every now and then it is good to feel the stomach grumbling because we have let it go empty." This is a very simple but very true way of indicating how we Catholics understand penance: penance both of the spirit and of the body, without excluding any component of the human being.

It is urgent that Catholic clergy get back to being wiser and more concrete on this, as on other points of our great Tradition. Just as liturgical worship is neither solely interior nor solely exterior, so also the spiritual life must include both dimensions, therefore not only the (true or presumed) mystical dimension, but also a very concrete ascetic one. Let us pray that the Holy Spirit will help us understand again that penance is important, that penance is good for us, and that true penance is above all that of the contrite and humble heart, but also of the body that is subjected to renunciation and deprivation.

The athlete trains the body thoroughly and subjects himself to all kinds of privations in order to win a perishable crown, says St Paul (*1 Co* 9:2, 5-27). Let us also, brothers, subject our bodies to some training. Under the guidance of a wise and prudent spiritual director, let us seek to undertake and perfect the practice of ascetic penance, and to inculcate it in the faithful as well.

Zeal for Souls: Choosing the Highest Goal of the Apostolate of the Priest

We conclude our Spiritual Exercises with this single morning meditation. First of all, let us recall today's solemnity of the Chair of St Peter, to confirm our filial sentiments towards the Petrine ministry which Christ intended to be compass, beacon, and guide of the Church on earth. The reflections we have already carried out also apply well to the ministry of the successor of St Peter. He is called to be for Catholics, and in some way for all men, a beacon of light. But this light does not come from him, from his personal abilities, refinement, ideas, talents. The pope, like any other priest but to an even greater degree, must shine. But he always shines with reflected light, and not with his own light. Like the whole Church, the pope too – we can say – must manifest the *mysterium lunae*. He is not the sun, because the true sun is Christ. He is like the moon that gleams and shines only insofar as it reflects upon us the rays of the light of the sun, which is Christ. The pope, in fact, is his Vicar, the one who must take the place of the Lord Jesus in the midst of the people of God, the one who does not speak for himself, who does not propose his own doctrine, but that of Christ. He must be like St John the Baptist, who does not draw attention to himself, but always points to the true centre, Jesus. He must make his own the words of our common Master and say, "My doctrine is not mine, but his who sent me" (*Jn* 7:16). So let us renew today our fidelity to immortal Rome, to that Rome, as Dante Alighieri says, "whereby Christ is Roman" (*Purgatory*, XXXII, 102). Let us fasten even more firmly the bonds of our Catholic soul to the Chair of St Peter, that Chair whose teaching has illuminated the centuries and millennia; that Chair which must continue to shine, reflecting the light of Christ, until the end of time.

As the theme of this last meditation, we have been entrusted with the following: *Zeal for souls: choosing the highest goal of the apostolate of the priest.* As you know very well, we talked about zeal for souls in a previous meditation, which is why we do not intend to repeat ourselves. But neither is it necessary to change the theme of this meditation, because it is possible to resume the discussion from a new perspective and by adding a few other reflections.

We have already said what zeal for souls is and why it is important. We now want to meditate on the fact that today the zeal for souls, the primary virtue of the priest, sometimes or even often seems to be hindered by the Church itself. Let us start with a fact that was made public by Cardinal Marc Ouellet in an interview a few months ago. The cardinal said that currently around 30% of those who are appointed bishops refuse the appointment. This means about three out of ten priests. How are we to explain this fact, especially since Cardinal Ouellet himself added that a few years ago, when he began his service as Prefect of the Congregation for Bishops, the average was much lower, about 10%?

There could be various explanations. Some commentators have said that this is a problem of faith, others have argued that those priests have sins (past or present) and are afraid that, once elected bishop, such sins could more easily become known. Both of these explanations are possible. However, there is a third that has also been advanced, and it is that today being a bishop seems to many a crucifying job without consolation. That is why many priests are afraid of it. They are afraid of losing the relative freedom they enjoy. They are afraid of always being the centre of attention, not to mention in the centre of the storm, especially when something negative happens in the local or universal Church. They are afraid of having to manage financial difficulties and cases of *delicta graviora*. And both of these situations are unfortunately becoming ever more frequent. In a word, these priests are afraid of the cross. On the other hand, it must be admitted that often the priests of their diocese do not support them either, nor does the Holy See back them in all cases. It is obvious that this is a very complex issue and that there are many different cases: from the case of an innocent and serious bishop who is, so to speak, unjustly "martyred" by the mass media, to the case of bishops who instead make themselves accomplices of sin or are even the authors of sin themselves. The array of cases is so broad and complex that it is impossible to say briefly here what would require extensive analysis.

In spite of this, it seems possible to say that there is a widespread perception among the clergy that being a bishop today is more difficult, more burdensome and complicated than in the past, and at the same time there is less help and consolation. Furthermore, at times one gets the impression that the bishop cannot act freely and autonomously even in his diocese, and has to depend entirely on the bishops' conference, whose official norms are established and clear, but whose concrete dynamics sometimes escape clear understanding.

Look, this could also be a valid explanation: a priest who is chosen as a bishop may be tempted to think: "Who is going to make me accept this? In my parish, or with my position in the curia or as a teacher, I am doing so well! At least in my current job I can do something good for the Church, while if I were a bishop I would be less in command and not more; I would have less freedom of action, not more." In human terms, these and other reasons can also be understood. They can be understood, but not justified.

We have all heard careerism condemned many times, and with good reason. A priest who does something to get himself promoted would not be showing zeal for souls, that is, love for the Church, but only zeal for himself. It remains true that many careerists who, due to their misguided aims, manage to become bishops, later complain not a little about the situation they worked to get themselves into! Then they would like to go back, but they cannot. So they think they have to keep moving forward, going higher and higher up the hierarchy. They delude themselves that in this way they will escape their present sufferings. They think, "If I got promoted to that position, then yes, I would actually be in charge!" Of course, careerism can also manifest itself without episcopal ambitions, as is the case with those priests who aspire "only" to have the best parish or the highest post in the Curia.

A wise priest used to say that a careerist is not entitled to complain. And this is because it was he himself who procured the reason and instrument of his sufferings. Instead, a non-careerist – that priest continued – does have the right to complain. If a priest has not done anything to reach a certain position and it has been assigned to him, and on account of that ministry he suffers, he has the right to present himself before Jesus present in the tabernacle to complain, as did Moses who spoke truly dramatic words to God:

> Why have you done wrong to your servant? Why have I not found favour in your sight, that you lay the burden of all this people on me? Did I conceive all of this people? Or did I bring them into the world that you should say to me, 'Carry them in your bosom', as the nurse carries the infant, to the land you swore to give their fathers? [...] I am not able to carry all this people alone, the burden is too heavy for me. If this is how you must treat me, kill me at once, if I have found favour in your sight,

that I may no longer look upon my misfortune! (*N* 11:11-12, 14-15)

The non-careerist priest can speak to Jesus like this: "Why, Lord, have you done this to me?" And the Lord pities him, because he knows that he gave him that cross and that the priest did not inflict it on himself. Therefore Jesus also replies to him, "My grace is enough for you; strength in fact is fully manifested in weakness" (*2 Co* 12:9).

Here, then, is another important point for the self-examination we make starting from these Spiritual Exercises and then also afterwards. It must be emphasised, too, that our examination on careerism must not be primarily an examination of desires (although in part it is that too), but of actions. We must not dwell only or mainly on the desire to become a bishop that may be in our heart. In a way, that is not the more serious problem. St Paul could even write, "If anyone aspires to the episcopate, he desires a noble task" (*1 Tm* 3:1). Of course, if someone desires in a disordered way he will probably behave accordingly, that is, badly. But even more than the inner aspiration, what really needs to be examined is whether or not we put careerist tactics into practice, if we do things because we hope to reap a promotion from them, and if we omit doing other things – however right they may be – because we are afraid they would compromise our ascent. So the examination is on the purity of intention with which I do some things or omit others. I may even have a healthy inner desire that Jesus would choose this unworthy sinner to entrust him with the undeserved honour of being a successor of the apostles (because that is what it is!) But this desire would be unsound if it blotted out the freedom to do good and avoid evil, if one began to act or not act on the basis of a policy of getting to an overriding goal: to advance a career!

And this fits perfectly with what we were saying at the beginning: it may seem that, in the Church today, true and healthy zeal for souls, instead of being encouraged and rewarded, is hindered (if not forbidden) and sometimes even punished. Revisiting the information provided to us by Cardinal Ouellet, we could also ask a question: 30% of those chosen refuse, but what are the criteria by which bishops are chosen? Are those selected orthodox priests, of holy life, truly courageous, balanced, zealous, full of the Holy Spirit and accustomed to prayer? Or are they selected because they are part of a certain group? Or are those chosen shaky on doctrine, even if they are very active in certain sectors of social life? Or again, among different candidates, is the best one chosen, or the one who is most diplomatic and – according to the current jargon – "least divisive"? These questions are also worth asking. The hierarchical Church, in fact, has the moral duty not only to provide itself with bishops, but also, if possible, to provide itself with good bishops. This moral duty is the consequence of the right of the faithful to receive good shepherds.

Furthermore, the hierarchical Church should do all it can to place the bishop (as well as the priests) in the best conditions for doing good work, with proper support, especially when bishops and priests are courageous, when they have the courage to proclaim sound doctrine by opposing worldly thought. And instead it is often precisely in these cases that zealous bishops and priests are left alone, if not weakened or delegitimised outright. On this concrete point too – as is evident – there are many different types of cases and one cannot generalise. But these are the "optics", as they say today.

Zeal for souls is the highest goal for the priest to choose: there is no doubt about this. But good priests must be supported in their zeal. Similarly, we priests must support and not hinder those good lay faithful who show holy zeal for the things of God and of the Church. Does it not often happen that the clergy encourage lay initiatives of a social nature, but then ignore or even hamstring those lay initiatives that instead propose a true evangelisation, an increase in liturgical worship, a perfecting of the moral life, a growth in the spirit of faith, prayer and devotion? Here is a second point of examination for us: I want to be supported in my own zeal, but do I support my fellow priests and the laity who have zeal themselves?

The situation today is quite difficult, but it is not desperate. A North American bishop gave an interview a few years ago, and he recounted some autobiographical details, particularly about the moment in which he learned he had been chosen as a bishop. He said that, on that occasion, he confided his perplexities and fears to a priest friend, referring precisely to the enormous difficulties that a bishop encounters today. And the one who had been chosen said to his brother priest, "This is a really bad time to be made a bishop." To which the other replied, "Then it is the right time to be a great bishop!" That is how it is, my dear brethren. The times are hard, but that does not justify surrender – on the contrary! And obviously this also applies to priests: it is a hard time to be a priest. Well then, it is a time truly right for great priests, priests truly zealous for the salvation of souls!

As we know, the philosopher Blaise Pascal wrote, "Jesus will be in agony until the end of the world; one must not sleep during this time" (*Pensées*, 553). Look, we are in the midst of a history in which Christ remains in agony. But this must not discourage us, it must not lead us to say: "Then there is nothing to be done." Let us remember the anecdote we have already recalled from the life of the Curé of Ars. They said to him, "You're too late, here in Ars there's nothing more to do." And he replied, "Then there is everything to do!" Let us roll up our sleeves, dear brothers, let us not waste our lives on idle matters, let us make good use of the time that Christ gives us. There is so much to do, so... let us get to work! Christ is in agony, this is true. And it is we priests who betray him, who crucify him again. But the consequence that Pascal draws from this is not, "Then let us sleep peacefully", but rather, "One must not sleep during this time". This is a thought based on the Gospel: Jesus rebuked the disciples in Gethsemane, because while he was in agony they were sleeping (*Mt* 26:40-41; *Mk* 14:37-41; *Lk* 22:46).

But let us return again to the point of meditation on which the whole discussion hinges: can we "not sleep", can we truly be zealous priests when it is often the Church itself that tries to block our zeal? Or at least, does the Church today seem to want us to be zealous for a certain type of work and activity, but seem not to want us to be zealous for others, for those more divine and supernatural?

This is an objection to be taken seriously. If a good priest wants better to promote the sacredness, beauty, dignity, and holiness of divine worship with legitimate and appropriate initiatives and certainly not on a whim, it is possible that his bishop may not appreciate this, may even reprimand him, hinder him, ask him to break off his initiatives. If a priest were to defend sound doctrine or apply canon law, in certain cases he could even be admonished by ecclesiastical authority. Here too the cases are many and varied: there are, in fact, also priests who are zealous, but in a disordered way. For example, let's take priests who post comments on the internet on doctrinal matters. Some of them defend sound doctrine, but resort to an inappropriate, exaggerated, disrespectful, or even offensive style and language. We have already said that the things of God are not to be spoken of in this way. In that case, if the bishop intervenes it does not mean that the bishop does not want sound doctrine to be defended. It could simply mean that the bishop is reminding his priest to do this the right way, that is, as St Peter puts it, with gentleness and respect (*1 P* 3:15). Or as St Paul says to the Galatians, "Brothers, if anyone is caught in some fault, you who have the Spirit, correct him with a spirit of gentleness" (*Ga* 6:1). But it is true that there are also cases in which the priest does nothing wrong, rather he does something good or even dutiful and in spite of this he is hindered or punished.

As for this, we must follow this criterion: as long as the Church does not formally forbid me to do true, good and just things, even if my bishop or my brothers are not doing them, it is my right and even duty to do them. Let us suppose that today many priests celebrate the Liturgy badly. As long as the Church allows me, with its norms, to celebrate well, I do so. Let us suppose that a number of priests teach erroneous doctrines to the faithful. As long as the Church has a Catechism that contains sound doctrine, I can and must adhere to that rule of faith and morals. And so on. Even if the authorities burn or ban the *Catechism of the Catholic Church*, they will not be able to burn my freedom, my conscience, and my faith.

However, we must know that this zeal can bring us the undesirable but foreseeable consequence of suffering. After all, prior to canonising her saints the Church herself always made them suffer, put them to the test, to see if they were serious, if they were truly sustained by the Spirit of God. Yes, the Church tests holiness not only with the posthumous canonical process, but already during life. The Church tests in the crucible, with fire, the rectitude of our intention, to see if it is sincere. The Church does this by making us suffer. And as unjust as this may often be, we must be willing to tolerate this suffering that comes to us not from external enemies but from brothers in the faith. We must accept the fact that some of the judgements, malice, negative interpretations of our work and spite may come from those who should support and encourage us. The consolation is that there are other brothers, both lay people and clergy, who instead help and support us openly and without fear, out of love for Jesus and his Church.

Faced, therefore, with the very difficult times in which we live, we priests must not lose but rather multiply our zeal for the salvation of souls. This is, in fact, the true, the only reason why we exist as priests: to participate in the salvation of souls. Whatever we do is, and must be, in view of this. Let us renew our zeal by remembering the words God spoke through the prophet Isaiah: "Strengthen the weak hands, and make firm the feeble knees. Say to the fearful of heart, 'Courage, fear not! Behold your God, vengeance is coming, the divine recompense. He is coming to save you'" (*Is* 35:3-4).

To you who have participated in these Spiritual Exercises I wish from my heart, dear brothers in the priesthood, that you may rediscover every day, in the encounter with Christ, this first love that prompted you to offer your life for the cause of his Kingdom. Turn every day to Mary Most Holy and to the great St Joseph, that they may teach you to serve Christ well – they, who did this with total dedication and absolute perfection. Pray also to St Michael, prince of the heavenly host, that he may keep away from you and from the faithful you care for the snares of the infernal enemy. Finally, invoke St John the Baptist, that just as he did so also may you, in a world largely dedicated to neo-paganism and moral and religious decay, point out to all men that the only salvation is in the Lamb sacrificed and risen, in Jesus Christ who offered himself on the altar of the cross two thousand years ago and who every day presents his sacrifice in a bloodless and sacramental form on our altars in our priestly hands. May your priestly work, inspired and guided by such great saints, be faithful and fruitful until that day when the book of this life will close and that of the other life will open, in which we all hope to be welcomed, hearing the words: "Well done, good and faithful servant [...], you have been faithful over a little, I will give you power over much; take part in the joy of your master" (*Mt* 25:21).